GO WEST!

CHICAGO AND AMERICAN EXPANSION

OLIVIA MAHONEY

CHICAGO HISTORICAL SOCIETY

The exhibition *Go West! Chicago and American Expansion* was made possible by these generous donors:

Leadership funding provided by :

A'A AmericanAirlines

Additional major funding provided by:

ARCHER DANIELS MIDLAND COMPANY

Additional funding provided by:

BANK OF AMERICA	PRINCE CHARITABLE TRUST
SARA LEE CORPORATION	THE NORTHERN TRUST COMPANY
LASALLE NATIONAL BANK	PHILIP MORRIS COMPANIES, INC.

Special thanks to former Governor James R. Thompson
for his efforts in securing funding for this exhibition.

Published in the United States of America in 1999
by the Chicago Historical Society.

©1999 by the Chicago Historical Society.

Director of Publications: Rosemary K. Adams
Edited by Lesley A. Martin
Designed by Bill Van Nimwegen

The text of this book is composed in Latin 725 by Bitstream with Onyx and Madrone display fonts.

Printed by M & G Printing, Chicago, Illinois.

Library of Congress Cataloging-in-Publication Data

Mahoney, Olivia, 1952-
    Go west : Chicago and American expansion / Olivia Mahoney.
        p.   cm.
    Published in conjunction with an exhibition at the Chicago
Historical Society.
    Includes bibliographical references and index.
    ISBN 0-913820-22-9 (pbk.)
        1. Chicago (Ill.)--History--1875- 2. United States--Territorial
expansion.   3. Frontier and pioneer life--West (U.S.) I. Chicago
Historical Society.   II. Title.
F548.45.M28   1999
977.3' 1104--dc21   98-53941
                                                                  CIP

For my family

Powerful tools of the industrial age, railroads were key to western expansion and economic development. An 1886 photograph captures a train crossing Minnesota's Red River Valley, one of the most productive wheat regions in the world with close ties to Chicago.

Contents

By 1870, Chicago had more railroad lines to the West than any other city. A map from an 1872 pamphlet entitled How to Go West shows lines stretching from Chicago (in the lower right corner) across the western half of the continent toward the setting sun.

Preface

The American West has long exerted a powerful grip on the American imagination. Frederick Jackson Turner's paper on "The Significance of the Frontier in American History," read at Chicago's Columbia Exposition in 1893, declared that "the existence of an area of free land, its continuous recession, and the advance of American settlement westward, explain[ed] American development." Turner argued that the movement west was the principal historical force shaping American character. Contemporary Americans may disdain the phrase "free land," recognizing that the West, like the rest of the continent, was occupied long before the first whites arrived there. Nonetheless, the image of "wide open spaces" has remained a compelling and sometimes disturbing theme in American cultural mythology. Over time, images as disparate as John Wayne in *Stagecoach*, Laura Ingalls Wilder living in a sod dugout on the banks of Plum Creek, a Georgia O'Keefe painting, or Huck Finn's expressed desire to "light out for the Territory" have amplified this perception. And, we should acknowledge, it has also found its expression in images of American Indians that range from the wildly romantic to the virulently racist.

Significantly, Chicago provided the setting for Turner's reading of his landmark paper, a paper that framed the study of the history of the West for most of this century. Chicago rarely appears in the mythology of the West, but as America's western-most urban outpost, it played a vital role in the realities of western history, the literal switch point for people, ideas, and commodities moving back and forth across the country. Chicago's factories made the windmills that pumped water for irrigation, the barbed wire that fenced in those "open spaces," and the farm machinery that reaped unprecedented agricultural bounty from the Great Plains. Chicago's lumber industry processed the forest products for western homes, schoolhouses, churches, and stores. And, above all, Chicago was the center of the nation's railroads, the interlaced lifelines of the West, carrying settlers to their new homes, bringing them the manufactured products of the East, and carrying back the agricultural products of the West.

This process not only altered the economic life of the country; it also transformed the nation's culture and sense of itself.

The darker chapter of Chicago's relationship with the West was that the city also served as the military headquarters of the U.S. Army's Division of the Missouri. The hunger of settlers for land pressed the army into astonishingly brutal military action. Under the supervision of Lt. Gen. Philip H. Sheridan and other veterans of the Civil War, the United States waged total war against the Plains Indians, eventually confining them to reservations and securing what Turner, not very much later and with no sense of irony, would describe as "free land."

Chicago even took a hand in the creation of the myths of the American West. William F. "Buffalo Bill" Cody began his show business career in Chicago. Chicago film companies made the earliest movie westerns, cranking out weekly hairbreadth escapes for this new medium.

This catalogue and the exhibition it accompanies document this chapter in Chicago's history. They do so not only because the remarkable collections of the Chicago Historical Society so richly support the telling of the story, but also because this is an American, as well as a Chicago story. Like the larger history of the country, the history of Chicago's role in westward expansion is both dramatic and ambiguous. In telling it, the Chicago Historical Society recognizes the city's unique and literally central position in America's past, present, and future. The results should simultaneously please and provoke readers and museumgoers alike.

In *Go West!*, Olivia Mahoney shows us how Chicago made the West and, conversely, how the West made Chicago. The era of westward expansion and conquest shaped the histories of the city and the nation alike. The advice of Horace Greeley, editor of the *New York Tribune*, to "Go West, young man," is well known. Less famous is the complete quotation: "Go West, young man, and grow up with the country." When America went West and grew up with the country, it went through Chicago.

Douglas Greenberg
President and Director, Chicago Historical Society

Introduction

Between the Civil War and World War I, the United States grew from a loose union of states, nearly destroyed by war, into one of the most powerful nations on earth. Driven by the forces of industrialization and nationalism then sweeping the globe, America's rise to power involved territorial expansion, political unification of its diverse peoples, and the creation of a strong central government. It also involved settling the great expanse of land that lay between the Mississippi River and the Rocky Mountains. To develop this region, Congress passed the Homestead Act, subsidized the construction of several transcontinental railroad lines, and obtained millions of acres of land for settlers through treaty negotiations with Plains Indians, confining them to federal reservations in the process. Together, these factors resulted in the rapid settlement of the West, and by 1890, the region had 8.5 million people—enough for the United States Census Bureau to officially declare the frontier closed.

Directly related to western expansion, the history of Chicago parallels that of the nation. A frontier outpost in the 1830s, Chicago had become an important industrial and commercial center by 1860 with vital railroad connections to eastern cities. After the Civil War, its burgeoning network of railroads reached out to the western frontier. By 1870, no less than four major lines linked Chicago to the transcontinental railroad, making Chicago the nation's leading gateway to the West. Capitalizing on new opportunities, Chicago's meatpacking, farm implement, and mail-order industries boomed with western trade that greatly contributed to the city's phenomenal growth. Strategically located between Washington and the western front, Chicago served as military headquarters of the 1870s Indian Campaigns, the nation's final clash with American Indians over control of the rich lands and resources of the country. Politically, Chicago became an important center of western protest against the role of big business in agriculture. In addition, travel guides, Wild West shows, and early cowboy movies produced in Chicago developed a romantic mythology about the West that became a central part of America's national identity, both here and abroad.

Published in conjunction with a major exhibition at the Chicago Historical Society, *Go West! Chicago and American Expansion* places Chicago within a larger context and relates its story to one of the most stirring chapters in national history. Yet, for all its excitement, "how the West was won" remains a troubling saga. Although national expansion spread the ideals and institutions of a democratic society across the continent and provided economic opportunities for millions of people, it also exhausted the hopes of thousands of settlers who failed to realize their dreams, and generated a long and bitter conflict with Plains Indians over western lands. As the Irish poet William Butler Yeats reminds us, the birth of a nation is indeed a thing of terrible beauty—while unity is achieved, it rarely occurs without conflict and loss.

Like other projects at the Chicago Historical Society, *Go West! Chicago and American Expansion* is an institutional effort and many people must be thanked for their contribution and support. The Historical Society's board of trustees, along with its director, Douglas Greenberg, enthusiastically supported the project from the beginning. Jay Frey, vice president of development and external affairs, and former Illinois governor James R. Thompson deserve special recognition for securing major contributions from American Airlines, Archer Daniels Midland, Bank of America, Sara Lee Corporation, LaSalle National Bank, Prince Charitable Trust, The Northern Trust Company, and Phillip Morris Companies, Inc. Special thanks, as well, to The Guild of the Chicago Historical Society for its help in promoting the exhibition.

Most of the materials used in *Go West! Chicago and American Expansion* are drawn from the Historical Society's superb and inspiring collection. I am indebted to the Historical Society's expert staff in the Collections and Research Division, past and present, for helping me locate the best materials. I would also like to thank my generous colleagues at several other institutions, as well as many private collectors, for lending wonderful artifacts for this project.

Russell Lewis, deputy director of collections and research, and Phyllis Rabineau, deputy director of interpretation, provided overall guidance for the project, while their dedicated staff carried out its implementation. Rosemary Adams, director of publications, Gwen Ihnat, Lesley Martin, and Patricia Bereck Weikersheimer edited the book and the exhibition labels. Using photography produced by John Alderson and Jay Crawford, Bill Van Nimwegen designed the book, weaving together material culture with historical narrative. Susan Samek, director of exhibitions, managed the exhibition's complex production, while Kathleen Zygmun developed engaging visitor interactives, selected materials from western institutions, and, with the help of Melinda Kweder, kept track of more than five hundred artifacts. Dan Oliver created an exhibition design that is sensitive to the history of the period and to the needs of museum visitors, with Julie Nauman providing complementary graphics. Steve Skinner headed a skilled team of installers. John Russick provided invaluable assistance in developing interactives as did Laura Kamedulski in co-ordinating the audiovisuals. Lynn McRainey, director of history programs, along with Heidi Gunther, Maria Lettiere, Marne Bariso, Andrew Montgomery, and Marie Haugh-Scatena developed challenging programming and interpreter training to accompany the exhibition. Very early in the project, Mark Turcotte created an exhibition database of information and digital images; registrar Julie Katz skillfully managed all loans, while Carol Turchan, Nancy Buenger, Tamsen Fuller, and Michelle Keim-Muller carefully conserved artifacts for exhibition. Cynthia Mathews organized photographic reproductions. Bernard Reilly and Ralph Pugh provided helpful advice on the manuscript, and Sylvia Landsman, with her usual good cheer and efficiency, performed countless tasks, from creating research files to entering corrections on the manuscript to ordering images from other institutions.

Several academic scholars served as consultants for the project, providing invaluable advice on the exhibition and manuscript: Raymond DeMallie of Indiana University; Craig Howe of the National Museum of the American Indian; Harvey Markowitz of The Newberry Library; Walter Nugent of Notre Dame University; and Carol O'Connor of Utah State University. In addition, Dr. Howe served as assistant curator of "Contested Lands," a major section of the exhibition that explores the history of Plains Indians during the late nineteenth century; his perspectives and contributions will help everyone reach a better understanding of this critical chapter of American history.

Finally, I would like to thank my family and friends for their support and encouragement over the past several years. I hope this story rewards them well.

Olivia Mahoney
Exhibition Curator

One of the most famous events in American history occurred on May 10, 1869, when officials of the Union Pacific and Central Pacific railroads drove a golden spike to complete the nation's first transcontinental railroad at Promontory, Utah. To signal the union, engines from the two railroads "touched noses."

ONE

Across the Continent

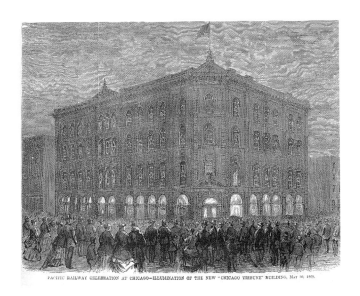

PACIFIC RAILWAY CELEBRATION AT CHICAGO—ILLUMINATION OF THE NEW "CHICAGO TRIBUNE" BUILDING, MAY 10, 1869.

As seen in the May 22, 1869, edition of Harper's Weekly, *Chicago celebrated the completion of the transcontinental railroad in grand style.*

On May 10, 1869, thousands of people gathered at Promontory, Utah, to witness the completion of the world's first transcontinental railroad. At exactly 12:47 PM, officers of the Union Pacific and Central Pacific railroad companies drove a golden spike to join the two lines. At last, a task that had taken seven years, thousands of men, and millions of dollars was done. When the news flashed across telegraph wires, Americans rejoiced, for the achievement not only confirmed their beliefs about industrial progress, but renewed their faith in the nation's future.

In Chicago, the celebration was especially grand. The courthouse bell, ingeniously wired to the offices of Western Union, rang out the news the moment it arrived. Fire alarms sounded while locomotives and steamships blew their whistles. Gurdon Hubbard, a prominent citizen who came to Chicago in 1818 as a fur trader, stepped off a parade of three thousand people that stretched for seven miles. Nearly fifty thousand people cheered the procession as it wound its way along Michigan and Wabash Avenues. As the *Chicago Tribune* observed, the day was "free from the atmosphere of war-like energy and suggestions of suffering, danger and death" that marked the Civil War years and seemed to be "full of peace and glorious in its promise of enlarged prosperity and happiness."[1]

All that evening, Chicago celebrated. In honor of the occasion, the *Staats Zeitung* and the *Chicago Tribune* illuminated their buildings with gaslight. The *Tribune*, a long-time champion of the railroad, proudly displayed the red, white, and blue emblem of the Union Pacific Railroad in its windows. Hundreds of people gathered at Library Hall to hear Mayor John B. Rice, Illinois lieutenant governor William Bross, and U.S. vice president Schuyler Colfax speak. According to Rice, Chicago had a special connection to the transcontinental railroad for "wherever the branches may be built and run, the eastern end of the grand trunk is in the city of Chicago."[2]

As Mayor Rice noted, Chicago had important connections to the West—connections that ran deep into the city's past. Nearly three hundred years before, in 1673, the French explorers Louis Jolliet and Jacques Marquette had identified the Chicago Portage as the critical link between the eastern and western halves of the North American continent. For the next one hundred years, the site served as an important link in the international fur trade, first controlled by the French and later by the British. As a result of the American Revolution, the United States gained control of the Great Lakes region and, in 1803, built Fort Dearborn to help defend its western frontier. Destroyed by a group of pro-British Potawatomi Indians during the War of 1812, the fort was rebuilt in 1816, but it remained an isolated outpost until the 1830s. The Illinois legislature then designated Chicago the eastern terminus of a new canal linking Lake Michigan to the Illinois and Mississippi rivers. Overnight, Chicago boomed with speculators and settlers seeking new opportunities. By the time the Illinois & Michigan Canal opened for business in 1848, Chicago had become a bustling center of trade and commerce with more than twenty thousand people.

Chicago's future, however, like that of the nation, lay not with canals but with the railroad. During the 1840s, railroads emerged as America's most important form of transportation. By moving people quickly over great distances, the Iron Horse revolutionized travel and linked the eastern United States together with a growing network of lines between major cities. As the country acquired more than one million acres of western land through the Texas Annexation (1845); the Oregon purchase (1846); and the Treaty of Guadalupe Hidalgo, which followed the Mexican War (1848), people started to imagine a railroad line across the entire continent, linking eastern cities to the West Coast. Although most Americans believed in Manifest Destiny, which claimed a

God-given right to spread across the entire continent, a host of troubling questions arose about the future. How could such a large country stay together? Would the slave system of the South, which held about four million African Americans in bondage, spread westward or would it be barred from this region as it had been from the Old Northwest Territory? Additional concerns surrounded Indian policy, frontier defense, transcontinental transportation, and communication. Moreover, many Americans doubted that anyone could live in the semi-arid region between the Missouri River and the Rocky Mountains, described by early explorers as a desert.

As debate over the western territories continued, it took on an increasingly sectional tone. While the western extension of slavery became the most explosive issue, the building of a cross-country railroad stirred controversy as well. Although most Americans remained skeptical, its fervent promoters argued that a transcontinental railroad, in addition to its commercial importance, would become a national highway of commerce and, by reaching the Pacific Ocean, link America to the lucrative markets of the Far East. But its route, financing, and management became points of disagreement.

Asa Whitney, a New York merchant who traded with China, submitted the first formal proposal for a transcontinental railroad to Congress in 1845. It described a line from a "terminus on Lake Michigan," later identified as Milwaukee, to the mouth of the Columbia River in Oregon, near the Pacific Ocean. To pay for the $65 million project, Whitney asked Congress for a land grant of ninety-two million acres of land that he would sell for $1.25 per acre. Although Congress took no action, Whitney's plan caught the public's attention and over the next several months, he traveled throughout the country, speaking to large audiences in Chicago, Milwaukee, and St. Louis.[3]

Despite its popular appeal, Whitney's plan had its critics. None proved more powerful than Illinois congressman Stephen A. Douglas. Originally from Vermont, Douglas moved to central Illinois as a young man in 1833. He entered the rough and tumble world of frontier politics as a Jacksonian Democrat and won election to various state offices before becoming a United States congressman in 1844. Proudly claiming that he had

Throughout his political career, Stephen A. Douglas served as a watchdog of the western territories. Although his plans for a transcontinental railroad failed to pass Congress, they laid the groundwork for its eventual construction.

"become a Western man," Douglas promoted a variety of plans to develop the West, firmly believing that territorial expansion would contribute to the larger goal of national greatness by extending the institutions of American democracy across the continent. Beginning in 1845 with his appointment as chairman of the House Committee on Territories and continuing throughout his career, Douglas served as the self-appointed watchdog of the western territories.[4]

Shortly after Whitney submitted his proposal to Congress, Douglas submitted his own, which differed from Whitney's on nearly all points. A route from Chicago, Douglas asserted, would be more "direct and natural" than a "circuitous" one from Milwaukee. He preferred California, a well-populated territory, over sparsely settled Oregon as the western terminus and considered Whitney's plan too expensive and self-serving. Furthermore, Whitney's plan would postpone western settlement, what Douglas called the "peopling of the country," until the entire line had been completed.[5]

Douglas called for official surveys to determine the line's best route and asked Congress to grant land in sections alternating between construction and settlement. Each state and territory would control construction within its own boundaries and settlers would each receive a tract of 160 acres. Douglas believed his plan would encourage an orderly occupation of the West, predicting that in time there would be a "continuous line of

As envisioned by its chief backer, Stephen A. Douglas, the Illinois Central became a major route of travel and trade. As seen in this view from Randolph Street, c. 1865, its right-of-way through Chicago ran along the lakefront.

Bridging the West

Building America's western railroad network in the late 1800s required spanning many western waterways, including the Mississippi and the Missouri Rivers. To handle the job, railroad companies often hired the American Bridge Company of Chicago. Founded by Lucius B. Boomer and A. B. Stone in 1851, the company built the first railroad bridge across the Mississippi River in 1855 at Rock Island, Illinois for the Chicago, Rock Island & Pacific Railway. A momentous event marked by celebrations across the country, the bridge revolutionized travel and trade across the Mississippi, hitherto crossed only by boat. During the Civil War, the American Bridge Company constructed many truss-type bridges for the Union Army. At war's end, the company turned west for new opportunities.

As the nation's railway network spread across the Great Plains, the company bridged the Missouri River at four different points for several different railroads: at Omaha, Nebraska; Leavenworth, Kansas; Boonville, Missouri; and Atchison, Kansas. In constructing these bridges, the company used a pneumatic process to sink iron and stone piers as deep as eighty-two feet into the loose, sandy river bottom. Its central headquarters in Chicago employed eight hundred workers at its 136,000-square-foot plant at the corner of Egan and Stewart Avenues on the city's South Side.

The American Bridge Co.'s Exhibit, U.S. Centennial Exposition, Philadelphia 1876, 2–3;

Chicago City Directory, 1876.

Lucius B. Boomer, c. 1876.

During the 1850s, the Galena & Chicago Union Railroad, Chicago's first railroad, thrived with western connections to Iowa, Wisconsin, and Minnesota.

rail roads to the Pacific" to serve the population. Douglas also proposed that mail, troops, and munitions be transported over national roads free of charge. Although Douglas lobbied hard, his plan failed to attract support in Congress.

After entering the United States Senate in 1846, Douglas became chairman of the Committee on Territories and continued to push for a cross-country railroad. In the fall of 1849, he presented a proposal to the Pacific Railroad Convention that called for a central route from Council Bluffs, Iowa, to the Pacific Ocean. To calm sectional rivalry, Douglas suggested that three branch railroads be constructed from Chicago, St. Louis, and Memphis to Council Bluffs. Although the convention elected Douglas president and eventually supported his so-called "Chicago Plan," they claimed it favored northern interests, especially Douglas's since he had recently moved to Chicago.

In addition to an East-West transcontinental railroad, Douglas's plans for national expansion and unification included a railroad that would bind together the mid-section of the country. Douglas envisioned this line converging with the East-West line in Chicago, making that city the undisputed capital of a massive transportation network serving the entire nation. Although sectional interests stymied his plans for an east-west line, Douglas succeeded in passing the Illinois Central Railroad Bill of 1850, with the help of Congressman John Wentworth of Chicago. The bill satisfied sectional interests by calling for the line to run from Dubuque, Iowa, to Mobile, Alabama, with a branch line to Chicago. It also provided for generous land grants to Illinois, Mississippi, and Alabama, making the Illinois Central the first land grant railroad in American history. Douglas's national triumph brought him personal fortune when he later sold some lakefront property in Chicago to the Illinois Central for a right-of-way into the city.[6]

The creation of the Illinois Central set off a frenzy of railroad building throughout the state. Employing large crews of predominantly Irish immigrants, the Chicago, Rock Island & Pacific Railway Company laid tracks across Illinois to the Mississippi River, reaching the "Great Father of the Waters" in 1854. In 1855, the company completed the first railroad bridge across the river, giving

the country an important new link to the western frontier. That same year, the Galena & Chicago Union Railroad reached Fulton, Iowa, on the Mississippi, forsaking
its original destination of Galena, in the northwest
corner of Illinois, for more lucrative markets in Iowa. By
1856, the Illinois Central had completed its line to Cairo,
while the Chicago, Burlington & Quincy Railroad was
operating an extensive rail network in Illinois and Iowa.
The decade closed with the formation of the Chicago &
North Western Railway under the direction of William B.
Ogden.[7]

Like Stephen Douglas, Ogden labored diligently to
make Chicago a great city. Originally from New York,
Ogden moved to Chicago in 1835. He invested in real
estate and became active in local politics, winning
Chicago's first mayoral election in 1836. In addition to
backing the Illinois and Michigan Canal, Ogden person-
ally funded the construction of more than one hundred
miles of city streets, as well as the first swing bridge over
the Chicago River at Clark Street. An energetic entrepre-
neur with an eye to the future, Ogden reorganized the
failed Galena & Chicago Union Railroad, resuming its
operations in 1848 with a profitable line to Maywood, ten
miles west of Chicago.

A firm supporter of western expansion, Ogden became
a national leader of the movement to build a transcontinental railroad. As president of the Pacific Railroad Convention of 1850, he championed its cause as "the great
work of the age" and encouraged the federal government
to fund the project. Like his fellow dele-
gates, Ogden believed that a transcontinental railroad would generate a
"more rapid diffusion of light and
knowledge," increase the "personal

*When it was absorbed by the Chicago & North
Western Railway Company in 1864, the Galena
& Chicago Union Railroad presented
a silver-plated lantern (top right)
to assistant superintendent E. H.
Williams for many years of
dedicated service. The lamp wick
trimmer (right) belonged to Ole A. McBride, a
station agent for the Chicago & North Western.*

relations and friendly feeling of the people of the same country" and promote "kindly intercourse and better acquaintance and understanding between the people of neighboring states and countries."[8]

The same could be said of a national telegraph network that Chicago helped develop. During the 1850s, Chicago became an important telegraph center, largely through the efforts of Judge John Dean Caton who founded the Illinois & Mississippi Telegraph Company. Contracting with all of Chicago's major railroad companies, the Illinois & Mississippi Telegraph Company quickly became one of the nation's largest telegraph systems with an extensive network of lines throughout Illinois, Iowa, and Missouri. A western expansionist, Caton belonged to the North American Telegraph Association headed by Hiram Sibley, president of the Western Union Telegraph Company. For years, the association promoted a transcontinental telegraph line along the route of the Pony Express between St. Joseph, Missouri, and San Francisco, California. Unable to raise funds for its construction, Sibley

appealed to the federal government. In response, Congress established the Pacific Telegraph Company to build the line, completed in 1861. When the Civil War broke out, Western Union took over its operation and also leased from Caton the entire Illinois & Mississippi Telegraph system.[9]

Thus, by the time of the Civil War, Chicago had become an important transportation and communications center. Although Chicago did not experience the Civil War directly, the conflict determined the city's future by establishing the course of western expansion. During the war, with southern opposition out of the way, the predominantly Republican Congress took up western expansion and passed the Homestead Act and the Pacific Railroad Act in 1862. The Homestead Act provided that any man or woman over the age of twenty-one who headed a family could obtain title to 160 acres of public land provided he or she lived on the land for five years and made improvements. Supporters viewed the act as a means to keep slavery out of the western territories by populating the area with northern farmers. The Pacific Railroad Act authorized the "construction of a railroad and telegraph line from the Missouri River to the Pacific Ocean." The railroad would consist of two lines, one built west by the Union Pacific Railroad from Omaha, Nebraska across the Great Plains and another built east by the Central Pacific Railroad from California. The Pacific Railroad enjoyed the enthusiastic support of President Abraham Lincoln, who, in his annual message to Congress, described the country's growing transportation network as being of "vital, and rapidly increasing importance to the whole nation, and especially to the vast interior region. . . . ."[10]

The Pacific Railroad Act officially created the Union Pacific Railroad Company, whose original investors included William Ogden and Henry Farnam, president of the Chicago, Rock Island & Pacific Railroad. Congress appointed Ogden, Farnam, and the other investors as the railroad's board of commissioners and called for its first meeting to be held in Chicago "not more than three nor less than one month" after the passage of the act. Con-

John Dean Caton of Chicago, an Illinois Supreme Court Judge, founded the Illinois & Mississippi Telegraph Company, one of the largest communications companies in America during the 1850s.

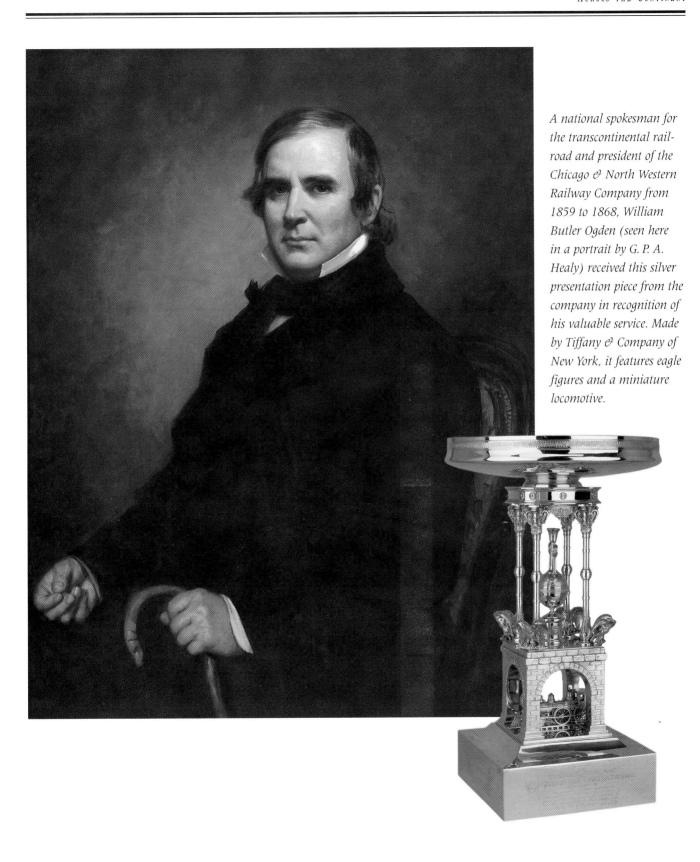

A national spokesman for the transcontinental railroad and president of the Chicago & North Western Railway Company from 1859 to 1868, William Butler Ogden (seen here in a portrait by G. P. A. Healy) received this silver presentation piece from the company in recognition of his valuable service. Made by Tiffany & Company of New York, it features eagle figures and a miniature locomotive.

gress also authorized board members to begin selling stock to private investors.[11]

On September 2–4, 1862, the Union Pacific Company held its first meeting in Chicago at Bryan Hall. About 74, or half of its 158 commissioners, attended the convention, electing Ogden as the first president of the railroad. In his address to the convention, Ogden praised the railroad but acknowledged the concerns of private investors who still considered it a poor risk. As planned, the railroad crossed a huge expanse of land still widely considered a desert where very few white people lived. Not only would its construction be difficult, but the line lacked potential customers. For many businessmen, the only commercial value of the railroad lay in its promise of connecting America to the lucrative markets of Asia, but that seemed remote and uncertain.

In reviewing the Pacific Railroad Act, Ogden declared the bill "substantially well drawn" but "patched a little" and suggested several amendments that would attract investors. Because the railroad would pass through private as well as government property, the Union Pacific Company had to have the authority to condemn land for the purpose of acquisition. In addition, the company had to be able to mortgage land to raise money for construction. Finally, Ogden urged that 7 percent of the railroad's earnings be distributed to stockholders shortly after the government started operating the road. Ogden believed that this plan was one that "capitalists will be glad to take hold of."[12]

Private investors, however, remained lukewarm and the slow sales of Union Pacific stock delayed construction. By June 1864, the Union Pacific had not laid a single mile of track, while the Central Pacific had made only slight progress with thirty-one miles of track between Sacramento and Newcastle. To jump-start the project, Congress passed the second Pacific Railroad Bill in 1864. Strongly supported by Lincoln, the amended bill doubled the amount of land granted for each mile of track laid from ten to twenty acres, an unprecedented act that eventually gained nearly twenty-one million acres for the railroads. Following Ogden's recommendations, the 1864 act also gave the Union Pacific and Central Pacific Railroads the right to "purchase, take, and hold any lands or premises that may be necessary and proper for the construction."[13]

Opposite: Abraham Lincoln, a long-time supporter of the transcontinental railroad, authorized its construction by signing the Pacific Railroad Act of 1862. Created by Daniel Chester French in 1912, this bronze statue is a smaller version of one at the state capitol building in Lincoln, Nebraska.
Right: Abraham Lincoln's personal set of transcontinental railroad surveys compiled by government surveyors in 1853–54. Although they failed to determine a route, the surveys compiled a wealth of new information about the West. Volume opened to a view of Sangre de Cristo Pass (located in present-day Colorado).

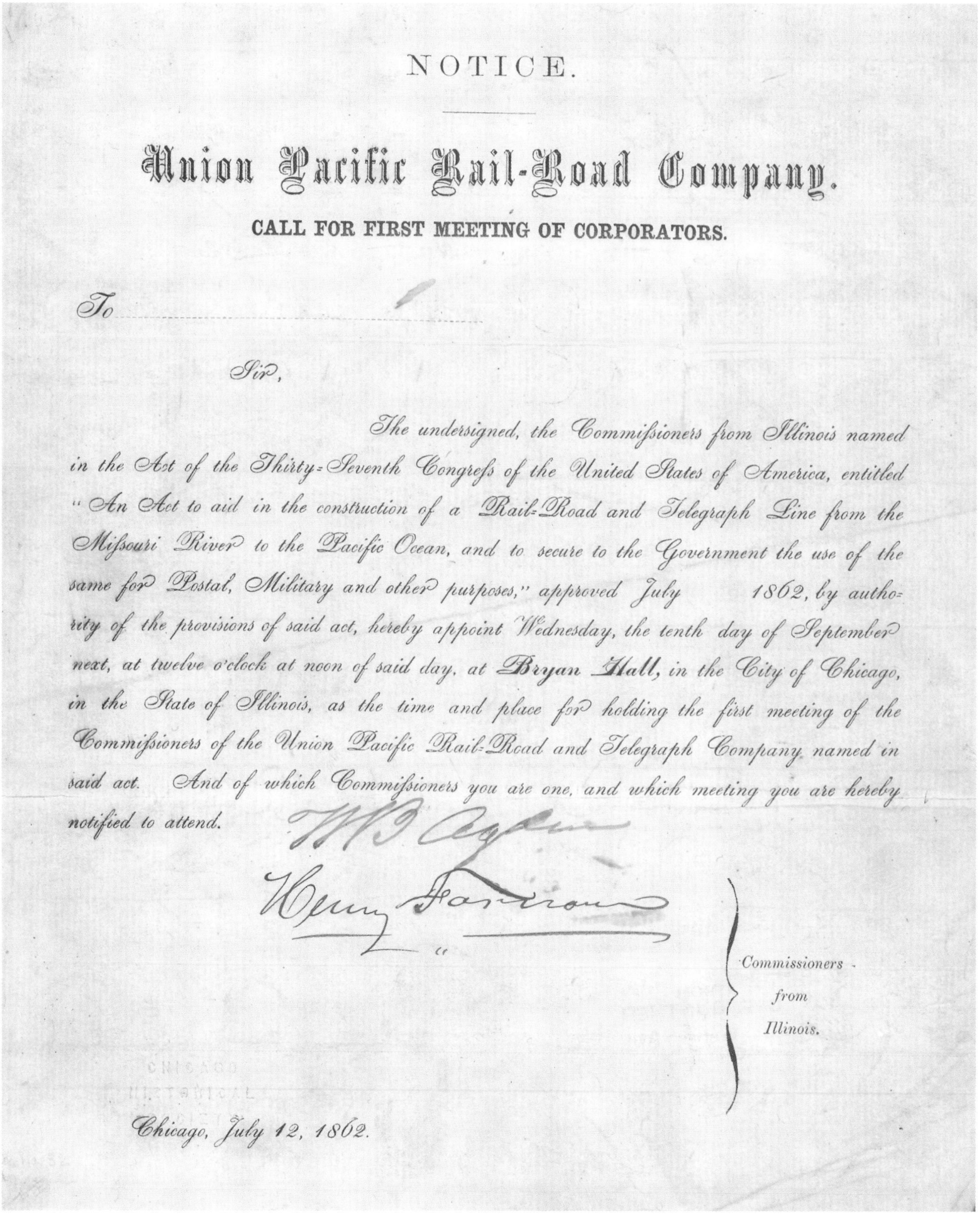

NOTICE.

Union Pacific Rail-Road Company.

CALL FOR FIRST MEETING OF CORPORATORS.

To _____

   Sir,

    The undersigned, the Commissioners from Illinois named in the Act of the Thirty-Seventh Congress of the United States of America, entitled "An Act to aid in the construction of a Rail-Road and Telegraph Line from the Missouri River to the Pacific Ocean, and to secure to the Government the use of the same for Postal, Military and other purposes," approved July   1862, by authority of the provisions of said act, hereby appoint Wednesday, the tenth day of September next, at twelve o'clock at noon of said day, at **Bryan Hall**, in the City of Chicago, in the State of Illinois, as the time and place for holding the first meeting of the Commissioners of the Union Pacific Rail-Road and Telegraph Company, named in said act. And of which Commissioners you are one, and which meeting you are hereby notified to attend.

      W B Ogden

      Henry Farnam
              } Commissioners from Illinois.

Chicago, July 12, 1862.

While financial difficulties slowed the construction of the transcontinental line, Chicago railroads surged westward, anticipating its completion. In 1864, Ogden, who resigned from the Union Pacific in 1863, merged the Chicago & North Western Railway with the Galena & Chicago Union to acquire an important network of lines in Iowa. At the same time, the Chicago, Rock Island & Pacific, the Illinois Central, and the Chicago, Burlington & Quincy railroads laid some track in Iowa, but the Civil War slowed construction. Not until after the war ended in 1865 did the race begin in earnest. Employing large crews of immigrant labor, Chicago's railroads engaged in a furious race to meet the Union Pacific, which had begun construction west from Omaha.

Further ahead and better financed, the Chicago & North Western beat all competitors. Arriving in Council Bluffs, Iowa, late at night on January 22, 1867, the crew found sixteen inches of ice covering the Missouri River. In a remarkable act of bravado, they quickly laid a line of temporary track across the frozen stream and drove the train into Omaha.

"All hail to our sister city of the West! May the union improve our humanity, secure our happiness, and advance our prosperity forever," telegraphed Mayor Rice to Council Bluffs, while its board of trade proclaimed that "the Garden City of the Lakes and the commercial metropolis of the Missouri slope are this day united in iron bands." Nearly three weeks later, the Chicago & North Western's first passenger train arrived in Council Bluffs, where it was greeted by booming cannons and a parade of citizens. As the only company with a direct connection to the transcontinental railroad, the Chicago & North Western began to ship construction supplies to the Union Pacific. Previously, all supplies had been shipped up the Missouri River to Omaha, then sent by rail to line's end. Whereas the shallow depth or frozen state of the river impeded traffic for all but three or four months of the year, the railroad could send supplies of wood and iron to the Union Pacific all year round, greatly speeding its construction.[14]

Opposite: A notice signed by two of its original commissioners, William B. Ogden and Henry Farnam, announced the first meeting of the Union Pacific Railroad Company in Chicago. Top: Water jug, c. 1865, used by crews of the Chicago & North Western Railway Company. Above: Commemorative pick and shovel used by officers of the Union Pacific Railroad to begin construction of the transcontinental railroad at Omaha, Nebraska, on December 2, 1863.

Built as a commercial route, the Union Pacific Railroad also provided access to some of the most spectacular scenery in the world. This view, c. 1870, is of Citadel Rock in the Green River Valley, Utah.

Construction of the transcontinental railroad wrote a memorable chapter in American history. Both the Central Pacific and Union Pacific railroads employed large crews that included Chinese, Irish, and German immigrants, Civil War veterans (both Union and Confederate), freed slaves, Plains Indians, Mormons, and basically anyone else who needed a job. They worked from dawn to dusk, receiving between $2.50 and $4.00 per day. At first, crews laid one mile of track per day, but during the peak of construction in 1868–69, when the Union Pacific alone employed ten thousand men, the workers hammered down six to seven miles per day in a grueling race to the finish.

The completion of the transcontinental railroad on May 10, 1869, marked a watershed in American history. As Stephen Douglas and William Ogden had envisioned, the transcontinental railroad became an economic lifeline of trade between East and West. In terms of human transportation, it provided millions of people with a quick and relatively inexpensive means to move west. Yet, it must be noted that the railroad, a major agent of change for all Americans, adversely affected the lives of American Indians who had lived in the West for generations by making their lands accessible to a huge wave of settlers and investors.

For Chicago, the completion of the transcontinental railroad ushered in an era of unprecedented growth with four major lines to the Union Pacific, three more than any other city. In addition to the Chicago & North Western, these lines were the Chicago, Rock Island & Pacific, the Chicago, Burlington & Quincy, and the Illinois Central. As a result, Chicago became the nation's most important "jumping off" place for millions of people migrating west over the next fifty years. These connections also gave Chicago unparalleled access to new markets, and over the next half century, its meatpacking, agricultural equipment, and mail-order industries boomed, quickly becoming the largest in the world. As the transportation and economic capital of the West, Chicago exerted considerable influence over its development and, in the process, became one of the most important cities in the nation.

NOTES FOR CHAPTER ONE: ACROSS THE CONTINENT

1. *Chicago Tribune,* May 11, 1869.

2. Ibid.

3. Sidney Breese, *Origins and History of the Pacific Railroad, the first report in Congress, 1846* (Chicago: E.B. Myers and Company, 1870); Robert L. Frey, *Railroads in the Nineteenth Century* (New York: Facts on File, 1988), 436–37.

4. Robert W. Johannsen, *Stephen A. Douglas* (New York: Oxford University Press, 1973), 16–35.

5. Robert W. Johannsen, ed., *The Letters of Stephen A. Douglas,* (Urbana: University of Illinois Press, 1961), 127–33. Stephen A. Douglas to Asa Whitney, October 15, 1845.

6. Johannsen, *Stephen A. Douglas,* 163–65, 305–17.

7. Frey, *Railroads,* 43–48.

8. Bessie Louise Pierce, *A History of Chicago,* vol. II (New York: Alfred A. Knopf, 1940), 52–53, 62–63; *Proceedings of the Convention in Favor of a National Rail Road to the Pacific Ocean Through the Territories of the United States* (Philadelphia: Crissy & Markely, 1850), 52, 67.

9. James D. Reid, *The Telegraph in America* (New York: The Derby Brothers, 1879), 239–45.

10. George P. Sanger, ed., *Pacific Railroad Act, 1862, The Statutes at Large, Treaties, and Proclamations of the United States of America from December 5, 1859, to March 3, 1863,* vol. XII (Boston: Little, Brown and Company, 1863), 489–98; Don E. Fehrenbacher, ed., *Abraham Lincoln, Speeches and Writings 1859–1865* (New York: The Library of America, 1989), 402.

11. Sanger, *Pacific Railroad Act, 1862.*

12. *Chicago Tribune,* September 3, 1862; James McCague, *Moguls and Iron Men: The Story of the First Transcontinental Railroad* (New York: Harper & Row, 1964), 62–63.

13. George P. Sanger, ed., *Pacific Railroad Act, 1864, The Statutes at Large, Treaties, and Proclamations of the United States of America from December 1863, to December 1865,* vol. XIII (Boston: Little, Brown and Company, 1866), 356–65.

14. *Chicago Tribune,* January 23, 1867; Maj. General Grenville M. Dodge, *How We Built the Union Pacific And Other Railway Papers and Addresses* (n.p., n.d.), 17–18; H. Roger Grant, *The North Western: A History of the Chicago & North Western Railway System* (De Kalb: Northern Illinois University Press, 1996), 30; Wesley S. Griswold, *A Work of Giants* (New York: McGraw Hill, 1962), 206.

Above: During the late 1800s, railroads conquered the West, then served as its economic lifeline for most of the next century. In Dalhart, Texas, crewmen climbed aboard the engine of a Chicago, Rock Island & Pacific train for a group portrait taken in 1910. Opposite: Cabinet cards from the late nineteenth century portray western settlers whose numbers exceeded eight million people by 1890. Equipped with tools of the industrial age, they settled the vast reaches of the Great Plains in a remarkably short time.

TWO

Industrial Conquest

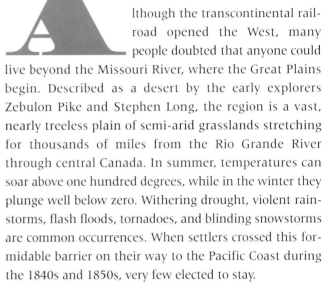

Although the transcontinental railroad opened the West, many people doubted that anyone could live beyond the Missouri River, where the Great Plains begin. Described as a desert by the early explorers Zebulon Pike and Stephen Long, the region is a vast, nearly treeless plain of semi-arid grasslands stretching for thousands of miles from the Rio Grande River through central Canada. In summer, temperatures can soar above one hundred degrees, while in the winter they plunge well below zero. Withering drought, violent rainstorms, flash floods, tornadoes, and blinding snowstorms are common occurrences. When settlers crossed this formidable barrier on their way to the Pacific Coast during the 1840s and 1850s, very few elected to stay.

Large-scale settling of the Great Plains did not occur until the 1860s, when Americans began to experience the full effects of the industrial revolution. The most powerful force of the nineteenth century, the industrial revolution had its origins in Britain during the late eighteenth century with the invention of the spinning jenny and the steam engine. The industrialization of America reached full throttle after the Civil War with the expansion of the railroad, the rise of the factory system, and the growth of cities. More than any other factor, industrialization made the settlement of the West possible.

Between 1865 and 1890, a great migration of people from the eastern United States and Europe moved to the Great Plains. Approximately four million strong, this "grand army of occupation" filled in the West with astonishing speed. By 1890, more than 8.5 million people lived in the West, prompting the United States Census Bureau to declare the western frontier closed. Still, the migration continued, and by 1910 more than twenty-three million people, nearly one-quarter of the nation's entire population, lived in the western half of the country.[1]

Notwithstanding the settlers' own courage and determination, this phase of American expansion would not have occurred without several key tools produced by an industrialized society, in particular the railroad, windmills, balloon-frame housing, and barbed wire fencing. Although industrial firms located throughout the country manufactured tools of western survival, those based in Chicago and its surrounding vicinity became the largest in the world. Along with the railroad, they rapidly transformed the "Wild West" into a settled region.

Chicago's role in settling the West begins and ends with the railroad. As the nation's rail center, Chicago served as the chief gateway for western migration. From Chicago, settlers boarded trains for St. Louis or Omaha and all points west. As western migration continued, Chicago's railroad industry grew at a phenomenal rate. Between 1872 and 1884, the number of railroad compa-

Above right: The depot for the Chicago & North Western Railway stood at the corner of Wells and Kinzie Streets. Right: The Chicago, Rock Island & Pacific Railway described its station at the corner of LaSalle and VanBuren Streets, as the "most convenient" in the city.

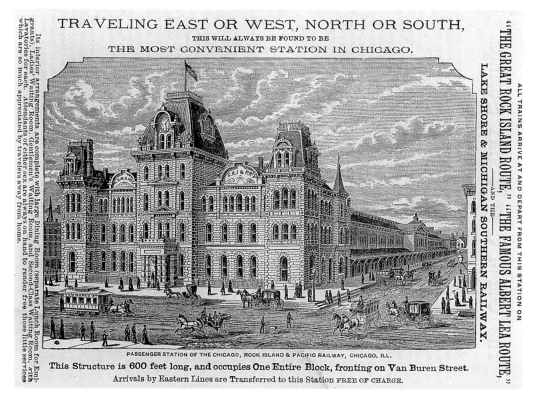

TRAVELING EAST OR WEST, NORTH OR SOUTH, THIS WILL ALWAYS BE FOUND TO BE THE MOST CONVENIENT STATION IN CHICAGO.

Its interior arrangements are complete with large Dining Room (separate Lunch Room for Emigrants), Ladies' Waiting Room, Gentlemen's Waiting Room, and Second-Class Waiting Room, with Lavatories for each. Attendants of either sex are always on hand to render free those little services which are so much appreciated by travelers away from home.

"THE GREAT ROCK ISLAND ROUTE," "THE FAMOUS ALBERT LEA ROUTE," —AND THE— LAKE SHORE & MICHIGAN SOUTHERN RAILWAY.

ALL TRAINS ARRIVE AT AND DEPART FROM THIS STATION ON

PASSENGER STATION OF THE CHICAGO, ROCK ISLAND & PACIFIC RAILWAY, CHICAGO, ILL.
This Structure is 600 feet long, and occupies One Entire Block, fronting on Van Buren Street.
Arrivals by Eastern Lines are Transferred to this Station FREE OF CHARGE.

nies operating in Chicago grew from seven to seventeen, and their profits increased from thirty to eighty million dollars overall. To accommodate nearly two hundred daily arrivals and departures, Chicago's railroad companies built huge passenger stations that dominated the city's landscape. By 1890, these included Grand Central Station at Harrison and Wells Streets; Union Central Depot on Adams and Canal Streets; the LaSalle Street Station at Van Buren and LaSalle Streets; and the Chicago & North Western Station on the corner of Wells and Kinzie Streets.[2]

Through these stations passed millions of people looking for new opportunities. For people living in the agrarian age of the late nineteenth century, this usually meant acquiring land, either through the federal government's Homestead Act or from railroad companies that owned vast tracts of land granted by the federal government. Although loopholes in the Homestead Act allowed developers to undermine its original purpose, this legislation provided more than one million people with land. To stimulate sales, railroad companies promoted the West as a new "promised land" of unlimited opportunity. Broadsides, pamphlets, and travel guides distributed throughout America and Europe lured potential settlers with glowing descriptions. The Chicago, Burlington & Quincy Railroad, which owned more than two million acres in Iowa and Nebraska, described the region as a farmers' paradise of rolling prairies and well-watered valleys, ideally suited for growing crops and raising livestock. The Chicago & North Western similarly stressed Iowa's excellent soil, pure water, and healthy climate. The company also emphasized Iowa's easy rail access to Chicago markets. To attract more settlers, Chicago railroads ran special excursion trains in the late summer and early fall so that farmers could see for themselves the abundant harvest. As an added enticement, railroads sold half-price "exploring" or excursion tickets that would be rebated to customers who purchased land from the railroad within thirty days.[3]

In an increasingly stratified society, railroads accommodated western settlers according to economic class. Wealthier passengers rode in luxurious first-class cars with dining quarters and overnight berths. Those holding second-class tickets rode in "good coaches" with dining

Chicago railroad companies sold western land to settlers at competitive prices. To encourage sales, they published fact-filled guides that promoted the West as a new "promised land," where hard-working people would prosper.

To increase its opportunities, the Chicago & North Western Railway Company sold land and tickets in the same office and published many guides to its "cheap" lands, including those in Minnesota and Dakota.

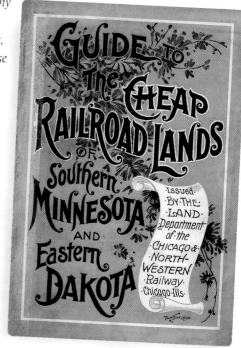

cars but no berths. For those of less means, railroads had "emigrant cars" where passengers sat on wooden benches with their parcels and boxes stowed underneath and cooked their own meals on a communal stove. A first-class ticket from Chicago to Denver cost about sixty dollars, a second-class ticket fifty dollars, and an emigrant ticket forty dollars.[4]

Although railroads provided settlers with a fast and fairly comfortable form of transportation, they faced a new set of challenges once they arrived in the West. Water, an abundant resource in the eastern states, became scarce as settlers moved further west. While many skeptics doubted that the Great Plains could be farmed successfully, immigration and real estate agents, railroad officers, and state officials assured settlers that "rain follows the plow," a widely accepted notion that cultivation of the soil led to increased precipitation. The *Chicago Tribune* reported on July 4, 1879, that in Kansas "the rain-areas are moving westward with advancing settlement, and that the requisite amount of rainfall may be depended on with as much reliance as in the Eastern States." The *Tribune* further stated that "this principle of

A Forced Migration

Long before white people migrated to the American West, the U.S. government forced nearly all eastern woodland Indians to reservations west of the Mississippi River. Officially adopted in 1825, the government's Indian removal policy was aggressively pursued by President Andrew Jackson during the 1830s. Among those removed were the Potawatami Indians of Chicago, who had lived in the area since the late 1600s. Like other tribes of the Great Lakes, the Potawatami practiced hunting and gathering along with some agriculture. When white settlers migrated to the area in the early 1800s, they encroached upon Potawatami territory and competed for its resources.

Rudolph Friederich Kurz's sketch shows a Prairie Potawatomi family taking the trail west in 1848.

During the War of 1812, Potawatomies sided with Great Britain and drove out American settlers by attacking Fort Dearborn. Twenty years later, when whites moved back to the area in sizable numbers, the federal government pressured this tribe, along with the Chippewa and Ottawa tribes, to sign the Chicago Treaty of 1833, ceding their territories in exchange for western reservations. Over the next several years, nearly seven thousand Potawatomies moved to reservations in Western Iowa territory and Kansas, while approximately four thousand left for northern Wisconsin and Canada. Despite the hardships of displacement, which included conflict with Plains Indian tribes on the western frontier, the Potawatomi Indians survived, maintaining a strong tribal identity and cultural heritage.

During the late nineteenth century, the West became a popular subject for American painters. Working in the romantic style, they depicted the West as a pristine wilderness of inspirational beauty, as in this 1871 oil painting, Rocky Mountain Scenery *by John H. Drury.*

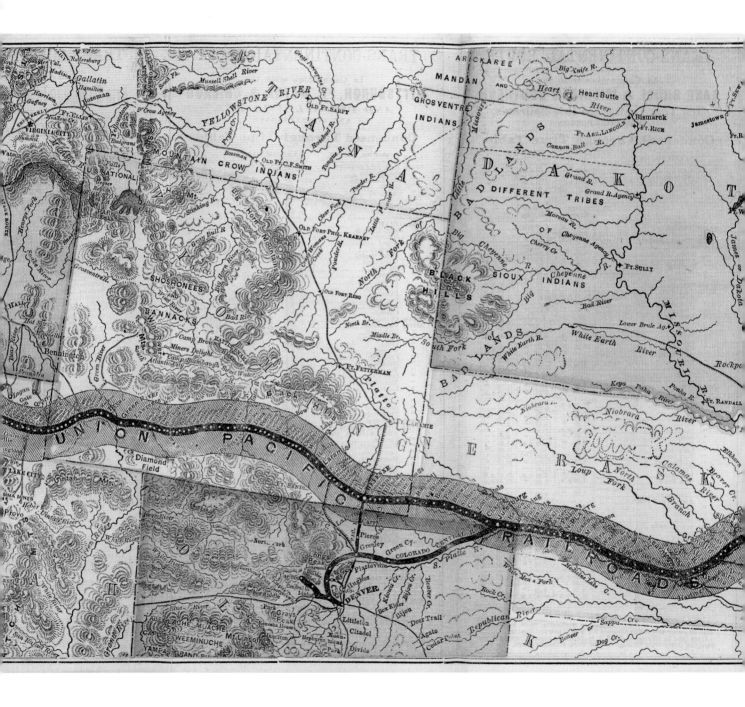

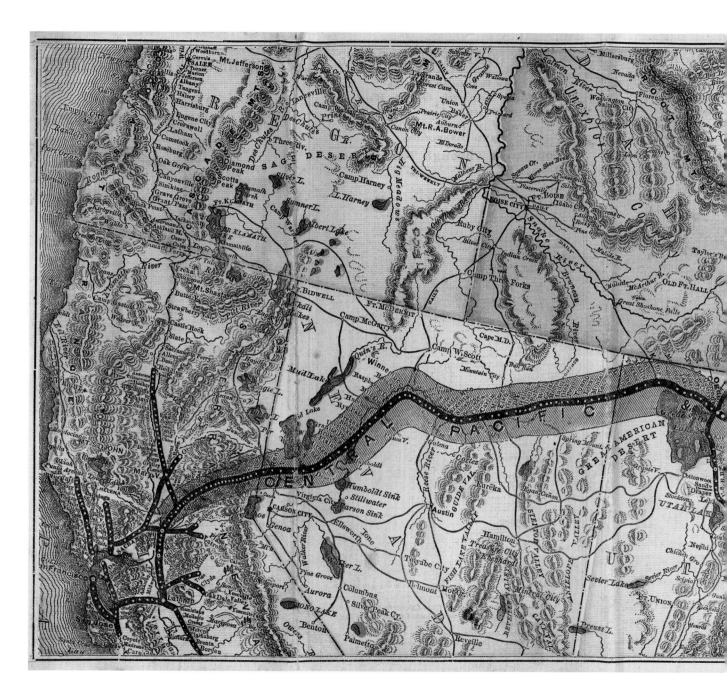

A map from around 1875 dramatically illustrates the Chicago & North Western Railway's vital connections to the West. The company had a direct route to the Union Pacific Railroad and an extensive network of lines across Wisconsin and Minnesota.

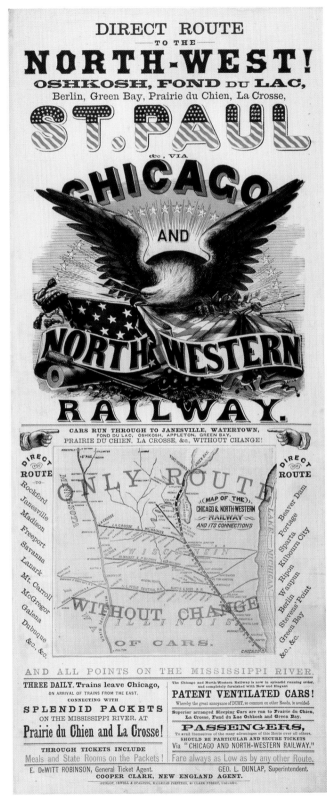

Colorful broadsides from the late nineteenth century announce routes and rates of the Chicago, Rock Island & Pacific and the Chicago & North Western railroad companies. Both companies made huge profits from western traffic, but they always earned more money hauling freight than passengers.

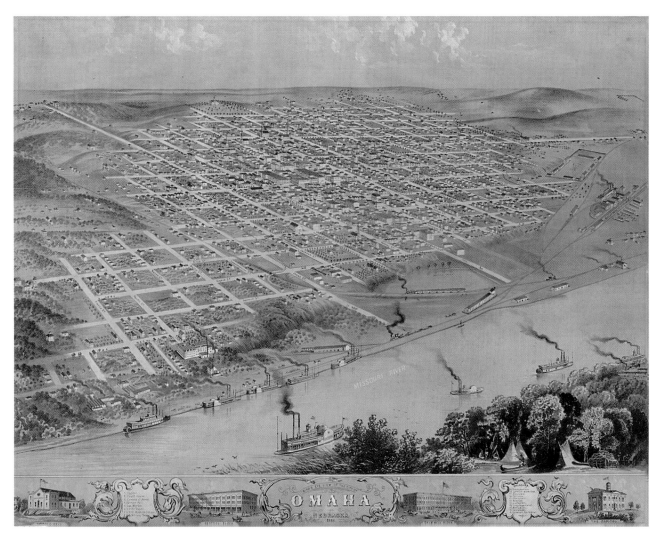

As the eastern terminus of the Union Pacific Railroad and linked to Chicago by several railroad lines, Omaha, Nebraska became a boom town after the Civil War. This lithograph shows the city in 1868. By 1890, its population had grown to 140,000, making it one of the West's largest cities. Left: A surveyor's compass reportedly used to lay out Omaha in 1854.

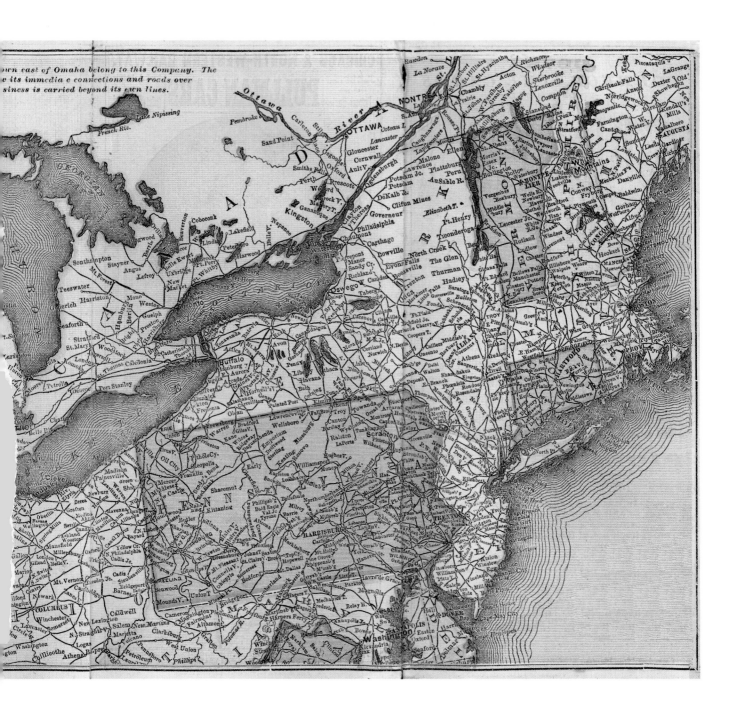

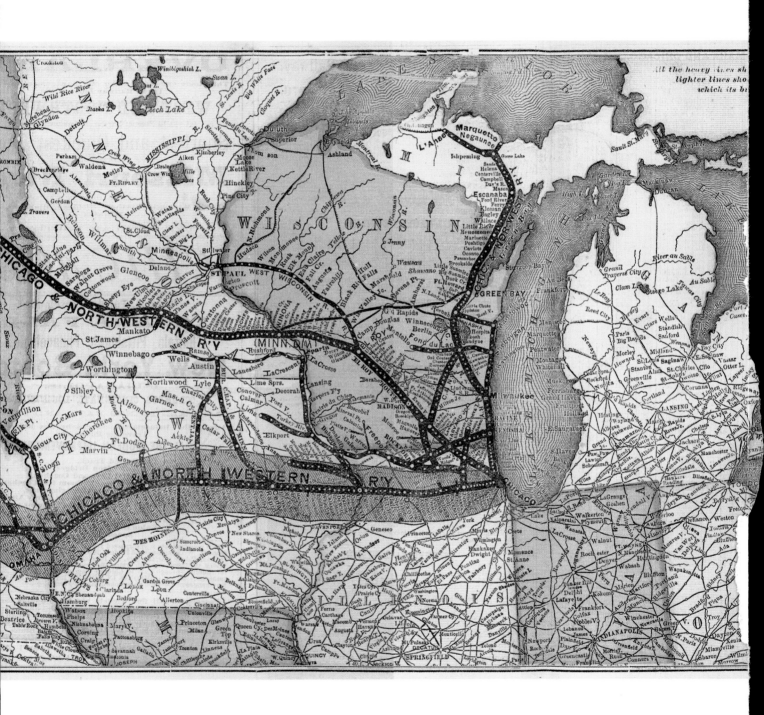

The U.S. Wind Engine & Pump Company of Batavia, Illinois, produced windmills sold throughout the West. Salesmen used colorful trade cards and small-scale, working models to promote their product at local stores and county fairs.

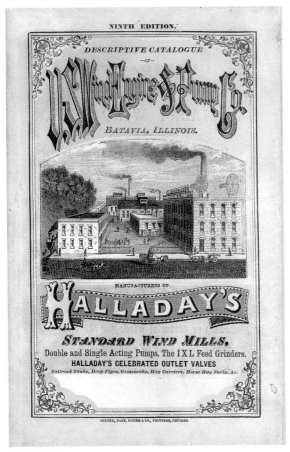

Catalogs published by the U.S. Wind Engine & Pump Company of Batavia illustrated their many uses, including that of supplying water for steam-powered locomotives. Customers included all Chicago railroads, as well as the Union Pacific.

rainfall accompanying settlement and cultivation of the soil is much more universal than was formerly supposed or understood."[5] For several years, rain fell in adequate amounts and the adage seemed to be true. Even severe drought during the 1880s failed to dispel the myth and in the early twentieth century, enthusiastic supporters of irrigation and dry-farming methods helped lure many settlers onto the High Plains, where rain rarely fell.

While a few communities, such as the Mormons in Salt Lake City, built shared irrigation systems, most westerners relied upon windmills to obtain water. Beginning in the 1860s, self-regulating windmills that pumped fresh water from below ground became a familiar sight throughout the West. This type of windmill used an ingenious system of rods and weights to incline the wheel away from increasing wind, thus preventing the wheel's destruction. As winds decreased, the wheel automatically returned to its original position.

Established in 1863, the U.S. Wind Engine & Pump Company, located thirty-five miles west of Chicago in Batavia, became the leading manufacturer of a self-regulating wooden windmill originally designed by Daniel Halladay. In addition to selling thousands of these windmills to western farmers, the company sold hundreds to railroad companies that needed water for steam locomotives. These customers included several of Chicago's railroads, as well as the Union Pacific Railroad Company, which purchased seventy giant sixty-foot models for its transcontinental line.[6]

Satisfied owners sent letters of praise to the company. John T. Flint of Waco, Texas, wrote: "I take pleasure in stating that the Wind Mill you put up for me about a year

Above: In addition to drinking water, windmills pumped water for irrigation, as seen in this view of a farm near Longmont, Colorado, c. 1900. Below: Made with interchangeable parts, Aermotor windmills were stacked and hauled in wagons by salesmen who also knew how to assemble and service their product. Opposite: An ad for Aermotor praises its tilting tower and pneumatic water supply system.

AERMOTOR COMPANY,
12th, Rockwell and Fillmore Sts.

ELEVENTH
ANNUAL PRICE LIST,
MAY 1, 1899.

CHICAGO, ILL.

SUPERSEDING
ALL FORMER
PRICES

ago, works well and gives entire satisfaction, pumping sufficient water to irrigate a portion of my garden, and furnishing a fountain with plenty of water. They are just the thing for this dry climate." F. M. Ross of York, Nebraska claimed: "I am a grateful 'Grasshopper Sufferer,' and would say to any one wanting a Wind Mill, get the Halladay, for it pumps with less wind than any other, and does not freeze up. I would not take $500 for mine if I could not replace it. I prefer it to all others."[7]

Chief competitors of the U.S. Wind Engine & Pump Company included the Challenge and Appleton companies in Batavia as well as Fairbanks, Morse and Company, which had offices in Chicago and a factory in Beloit, Wisconsin. The Aermotor Company of Chicago, however, soon outstripped them all by producing the first all-metal, self-regulating windmill. Established in 1888 by Thomas O. Perry and LaVerne Noyes, the company manufactured a windmill designed by Perry. It featured a back gear that made its action 90 percent more efficient than wooden types. As another unique feature, Aermotor towers could be tilted down so that the windmill fan nearly touched the ground, allowing the owner to repair the machine without having to climb the tower. With "the tower you don't have to climb" and "the wheel that runs when all others stand still," Aermotor boasted its windmill would "last as long with neglect as with attention, if you won't forget to oil it."[8]

High in quality, yet inexpensive to produce and purchase, the Aermotor quickly became the industry standard. In its first year of operation, Aermotor sold forty-five windmills. Two years later, it sold more than six thousand machines, and by 1892 sales reached sixty thousand. "Where one goes others follow, and we take the country," claimed the company and, indeed, by the turn of the century, Aermotor controlled half the national market.[9]

In addition to water, western settlers needed wood for shelter. A scarce resource on the Great Plains, wood had to be brought in from the eastern United States. To meet the growing demand of the 1870s, Chicago lumber companies heavily logged the virgin pine forests of northern Michigan and Wisconsin and sent stacks of finished lumber to Iowa, Kansas, and Nebraska, areas then being settled at a rapid pace. Western expansion, along with a

The Aermotor Pneumatic Water Supply System enables you to supply every part of your house with water without an Elevated Tank.

THE AERMOTOR CO.

GALVANIZED

After being completed the Steel Aermotor and Steel Tower are galvanized—absolutely protected from rust and decay. It is not enough to make portions of the wheel of galvanized Sheet Metal. That leaves edges exposed and is not so good as painting. The finished parts, galvanized together, make the whole practically one piece and exclude air, dampness and rust from all surfaces and places where two pieces of metal are joined. Our extensive galvanizing works, though an expensive necessity, perfect and complete the Aermotor.

AERMOTOR

THE STEEL TILTING TOWER.

Interior views of the woodworking department (left) and assembly room (above) at the Challenge Windmill Company in Batavia, Illinois, c. 1900, illustrate the industrial muscle behind western settlement. Like other tools of western survival, windmills were mass-manufactured in mechanized factories that seemed worlds apart from the western frontier.

building boom in the Midwest, made Chicago's lumber industry the largest in the world.

In the late nineteenth century, the vast majority of western settlers used this lumber to build balloon-frame structures. A revolutionary type of construction developed in Chicago, it used lightweight, machine-planed lumber and machine-made nails instead of the heavy, hand-hewn timbers and hand-carved mortise-and-tenon joints associated with traditional building methods. St. Mary's Church in Chicago, built in 1833 by Augustine D. Taylor, is recognized as the first balloon-frame structure. Several decades passed before the balloon frame caught on in rural areas where farmers adhered to more traditional methods. As the nation expanded westward, however, the new method spread across the upper Midwest and Great Plains, where settlers needed shelter in a hurry.[10]

A skilled carpenter with just one assistant could erect a balloon-frame home in about one week, compared to a seven-man crew and several weeks for mortise-and-tenon structures. Carlton C. Calkins, who moved from Chicago to Longmont, Colorado, in 1871, reported that he and another man built a fourteen- by twenty-foot frame house for about $240. Although Calkins admitted that his three-room house seemed "rather small by Eastern standards," he believed that it was "plenty large and as comfortable a home as one could desire."[11]

Ever ready with a new product, Chicago supplied western settlers with pre-fabricated balloon-frame structures. The Lyman Bridges Company of Chicago, with three warehouses in the heart of the lumber district, sold buildings of "any style, size, or number" on "short notice" to western settlers. Maj. Lyman Bridges, founder of the company and a Civil War veteran, arrived in Chicago in 1865. Within a few years, he had established himself as a "dealer in building materials" and in 1869, he began to sell ready-made houses, one-room schoolhouses, churches, military barracks, and railroad depots. Shipped by rail, the building kits contained milled lumber, building plans, roofing shingles, window frames, doors, hardware, and chimneys. The smallest, one-room house measured ten by twelve feet, while the largest home had two stories with eight rooms, pantry, china closet, hall, bathroom, and four closets. Prices ranged from $175 for the one-room house to $3,500 for the eight-room model.[12]

The West's lack of wood gave rise to another Chicago product: pre-fabricated, balloon-frame housing made with machine-planed lumber. The Lyman Bridges Company sold dozens of structures, all deliverable by rail within two weeks. Below: A single-story house such as this would have cost approximately $175 through Bridges.

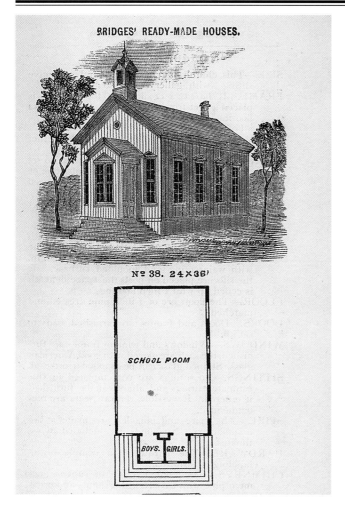

BRIDGES' READY-MADE HOUSES.

Nº 38. 24×36'

SCHOOL ROOM

BOYS. GIRLS.

To entice prospective customers, the Bridges catalog included sketches and floor plans of each building type, including one-room schoolhouses (above) and two-story homes (below). Such buildings became familiar sights throughout the West during the late nineteenth century.

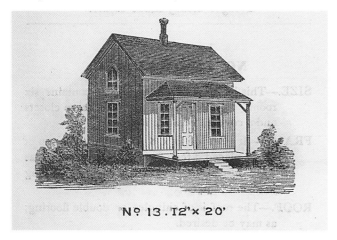

Nº 13. 12'× 20'

Pre-fabricated structures like those supplied by Lyman Bridges not only provided shelter, but comfort and style at an affordable price. Although far removed from eastern cities, western settlers strove to keep up with the latest Victorian fashions in housing, most typically Gothic style or, for wealthier clients, Italianate. Versatility, ease, and above all, affordability made balloon-frame construction the nearly universal preference of middle class westerners in urban, as well as rural, areas. As noted by Bridges, comfort, economy, and ease remained the primary factors in constructing a home.[13]

The West's lack of wood gave rise to another important tool of settlement: barbed-wire fencing. During the late 1860s and the 1870s, dozens of inventors, many of them living in Illinois and Iowa, patented more than four hundred different types of barbed wire. Joseph F. Glidden of De Kalb, Illinois, was among the most successful with his version, known as "The Winner." Together with Isaac L. Ellwood, Glidden established The Barb Fence Company, but soon sold his share for $60,000 plus royalties to Ellwood and the Washburn & Moen Manufacturing Company of Worcester, Massachusetts, a leading manufacturer of smooth wire fencing. In their new partnership, Washburn & Moen serviced the eastern states, while Ellwood's firm became the sole agent for the West and Southwest.[14]

Ellwood identified the Texas Panhandle as a primary market. By the late 1870s, settlers had moved onto its open range and Ellwood's salesmen, Henry B. Sandborn and John W. Gates, made frequent visits to the area, pitching their product to farmers and local hardware merchants. In 1881, Sandborn and Glidden established the Frying Pan Ranch on 125,000 acres and, at a cost of $39,000, strung 150 miles of wire around the ranch to enclose nearly sixteen hundred head of cattle. The ranch, they hoped, would demonstrate the benefits of barbed wire to western cattlemen who resisted the new product because it restricted their access to grazing lands and injured cattle. Although disputes over barbed wire erupted into the famous "range wars" of the early 1880s, cattlemen eventually accepted barbed wire because it gave them an inexpensive means to defend their land claims and contain their valuable livestock.

By the mid-1880s, barbed wire enjoyed widespread use throughout the West. Satisfied customers, like J. C. Boer

Lacking a ready supply of wood, westerners quickly adopted barbed wire as a means to mark property lines and contain livestock. Its various uses are illustrated on the cover of an 1884 catalog from the I. L. Ellwood & Company of De Kalb, Illinois, which became the largest barbed wire manufacturer in the world. Right: A few samples of barbed wire, c. 1880.

Vol. V. 1884. No. 5.

THE GLIDDEN Barb-Fence JOURNAL

I. L. ELLWOOD & CO.
PROPRIETORS
DE KALB, ILL.

of Nebraska, wrote glowing testimonials to Ellwood: "I have a pasture of twenty-five acres that I enclosed last season. I am well pleased with it, and say I believe it to be all that you claim, a cheap and reliable fence, and a necessity in this country." A hardware merchant in San Antonio, Texas: "[the wire] is nearly all sold out. It seems to be much in favor. Please ship us a car-load immediately to Kingsbury, the railroad terminus."[15]

In addition to an expanding agricultural market, Ellwood pitched its product to the railroads. As railroads expanded westward, they faced the challenge of enclosing thousands of miles of right-of-way. Along with wild animals, domestic cattle, horses, and hogs frequently wandered onto the tracks and into the path of oncoming trains. Western farmers and ranchers suffered high losses, often suing the railroads at inflated rates. Moreover, wandering livestock posed a constant threat of derailment and the loss of human life. To remedy the situation, western states required that railroads enclose their property. Faced with an enormous cost if they used wood, which also posed a considerable fire hazard, railroads chose barbed wire and became one of its major consumers.[16]

The widespread use of products like barbed wire, prefabricated housing, and windmills on the frontier demonstrates how quickly the "Wild West" became an industrialized region. An excellent example is the town of Longmont, Colorado. Located forty miles north of Denver, Longmont was founded in 1871 by the Chicago-Colorado Company, a real estate venture organized by Cyrus N. Pratt of the National Land Company in Chicago, a subsidiary of the Kansas Pacific Railroad. Chicago investors included William Bross, an editor at the *Chicago Tribune*; H. D. Emery, editor of the *Prairie Farmer*; and dry goods merchant George S. Bowen. Thanks to an aggressive advertising campaign, the company's membership rolls grew quickly, with more than three hundred people from Illinois, Colorado, Massachusetts, and several other states joining at a cost of $155 each.[17]

Settlers began to arrive in March 1871 and by June, Longmont had a population of four hundred people. Organized as a semi-cooperative venture, like the nearby town of Greeley, the colony purchased and distributed real estate lots and dug the irrigation ditches critical to

As recorded in an original plan from 1871, the Chicago colony of Longmont, Colorado, included a central main street, surrounded by residential areas and several parks. Although plans for a lake and university never materialized, the town thrived, largely due to its important railroad connections.

maintaining an adequate water supply. Arranged in a typical grid pattern, the town consisted of a central main street and business district, residential areas, and several sections reserved for parks, schools, churches, and county buildings. A two-story balloon-frame structure served as Longmont's town hall, as well as its library and temporary school. Like many western towns, Longmont grew quickly and within a year of its founding, had twenty miles of canals, a bank, a flour mill, a newspaper, and many small businesses. Longmont also struggled with financial problems stemming from illegal land sales along with devastating spring floods and summer grasshopper plagues.[18] But unlike many western towns

St Vrain Block *Longmont Colorado 1872*
East side of Main Street

Above: In 1872, Longmont had the typical appearance of a frontier town with a few frame buildings like the St. Vrain Hotel. Nearly destroyed by fire in 1879, the town quickly rebuilt itself and by the late 1800s (below) it had become a thriving commercial center.

By 1900, Longmont had a mixed farm and industrial economy linked to a national market by the railroad. In addition to the "Pride of the Rockies" flour mill (above), Longmont boasted an ore mill, a vegetable cannery, and a quarry.

that disappeared within a few years, Longmont survived such challenges primarily because it quickly acquired the most important tool of western expansion—the railroad.

In 1873, just two years after Longmont's founding, the Colorado Central Railroad connected the settlement to the booming Golden-Denver area. Four years later, the Union Pacific Railroad extended the Colorado Central line north from Longmont to its own line six miles west of Cheyenne. Longmont's rail connections linked the small community to a national market and brought its residents the latest news, fashion, and consumer goods on a regular basis. Businesses located in Denver, Cincinnati, St. Louis, and Chicago advertised in Longmont newspapers and sold their goods through local merchants.

Chicago advertisers included the Schuttler Wagon Company, the J. M. Brunswick billiard table company, and the Chicago, Rock Island & Pacific Railroad Company. As a route of commerce and trade, railroads also gave Longmont farmers access to the larger urban markets where they could sell their grain, produce, and livestock.[19]

Because of the railroad, Longmont thrived. By 1878, bank transactions exceeded $1 million dollars, flour manufacturing produced $250,000 dollars, and hay, feed, and grain sales netted nearly $140,000 dollars. *Crofutt's New Overland Tourist Guide,* the most popular western travel guide in America, recognized Longmont as "one of the most important towns on the railroad line. . . . During the last year, over 300 carloads of wheat were shipped from

Longmont, besides what was ground in three mills located near the town. . . . Its population is about 800, and rapidly increasing."[20]

Then, on September 8, 1879, disaster struck. At one o'clock in the morning, a fire started in Longmont's bakery. Flames quickly spread next door to the hotel and drug store and soon engulfed most of the balloon-frame buildings on the east side of Main Street. Since Longmont did not have a fire-fighting company, volunteers formed a bucket brigade from the town pump and creek. When they finally quenched the flames, an entire city block lay in ruins.

The Big Fire, as it became known, caused $50,000 worth of damage, but Longmont, like Chicago after the Great Fire of 1871, quickly rebuilt itself. City trustees passed an ordinance stating that "all outside and party walls shall be made of stone, brick, concrete or other fireproof material," and within a few months, several brick structures lined Main Street. Over the next decade, Longmont became more of an industrial center with an ore mill, a grain elevator, a vegetable cannery, and a quarry. These new industries attracted people from rural areas, where mechanization continuously reduced the need for labor.[21]

While unique in its own way, Longmont's history is typical of hundreds of western towns that grew as a result of the industrial revolution and its greatest harbinger, the railroad. No place, large or small, escaped the effects of these powerful forces and no history of the West is complete without including them.

NOTES FOR CHAPTER TWO: INDUSTRIAL CONQUEST

1. Allan G. Brogue, "An Agricultural Empire," *The Oxford History of the American West*, ed. Clyde A. Milner II, Carol A. O'Connor, and Martha A. Sandweiss (New York: Oxford University Press, 1994), 296–97.

2. A. T. Andreas, *History of Chicago, From the Earliest Period to the Present Time,* vol. III (Chicago: A. T. Andreas Company, 1886), 189.

3. *Hand Book and Guide to 1,200,000 Acres of Iowa Land in the Middle Region of Western Iowa and 35,000 Acres in Eastern Nebraska* (Cedar Rapids, Iowa: Times Steam Printing House, 1877), 32.

4. *Harper's Weekly*, November 13, 1886; *How to Go West/Guide to Iowa, Nebraska, Kansas, California, and the Great West* (Chicago: Horton & Leonard, 1872), 65.

5. *Chicago Tribune*, July 4, 1879.

6. T. Lindsay Baker, *A Field Guide to American Windmills* (Norman, Oklahoma: University of Oklahoma Press, 1985), 316–17; Volta Torrey, *Wind-Catchers: American Windmills of Yesterday and Tomorrow* (Brattleboro, Vermont: The Stephen Green Press, 1976), 96.

7. *Descriptive Catalog, U.S. Wind Engine and Pump Co.* (Chicago: Culver, Page, Hoyne & Co., Printers, 1878), 14–15.

8. *Aermotor 15th Annual Descriptive Catalog*, (Chicago: The Aermotor Company, 1903), 13.

9. Baker, 3–4, 114–17.

10. Fred W. Peterson, *Homes in the Heartland: Balloon Frame Farmhouses of the Upper Midwest, 1850–1920* (Lawrence, Kansas: University Press of Kansas, 1992), 8–11.

11. manuscript, Carleton Chase Calkins, June 29, 1871.

12. *Lyman Bridges Building Materials and Ready Made Houses* (Chicago: Rand, McNally & Co., 1870), 1.

13. Ibid., 5.

14. Henry D. McCallum and Frances T. McCallum, *The Wire That Fenced the West* (Norman, Oklahoma: University of Oklahoma Press, 1965), 115–20.

15. Washburn & Moen Mfg. Co. and I. L. Ellwood & Co., *The Utility, Efficiency, and Economy of Barb Fence* (Worcester, Mass.: Noyes, Snow & Co., 1877), 23, 28.

16. McCallum and McCallum, *The Wire That Fenced*, 199–201.

17. James F. Willard and Colin B. Goodykoontz, ed., "Experiments in Colorado Colonization, 1869–1872," from *The University of Colorado Historical Collections*, vol. III, 139–43, 160–201; St. Vrain Historical Association, *They Came to Stay* (Longmont Printing Co., 1971), 1–3.

18. St. Vrain Historical Association, *They Came to Stay*, 273.

19. Ibid., 271–72;. Richard C. Overton, *Gulf to Rockies: The Heritage of the Fort Worth and Denver-Colorado and Southern Railways, 1861–1898* (Austin: University of Texas Press, 1953), 17.

20. St. Vrain Historical Association, *They Came to Stay*, 273; *Crofutt's New Overland Tourist and Pacific Coast Guide* (Chicago: The Overland Publishing Co.), 66.

21. *The Longmont Ledger*, September 8, 1879.

U. S. Army soldiers marching in pursuit of Sioux Indians in Montana Territory, c. 1876.

THREE

War Without

Although American expansion created new opportunities for millions of people, it also generated a bitter conflict with Plains Indians over the use and control of western lands. Chicago's connection to this dark chapter of western history began on April 1, 1869, when it replaced St. Louis as the headquarters of the U.S. Army's Division of the Missouri, a huge area that encompassed the Great Plains. By then, Chicago had superb railroad and telegraph connections to this region, where approximately 175,000 American Indians lived. Their numbers included between forty and fifty thousand woodland Indians belonging to dozens of tribes, including the Delaware, Cherokee, Choctaw, Chickasaw, Creek, Seminole, Fox, Miami, and Potawatomi. During the early 1800s, these tribes had been removed from the eastern United States by the federal government to secure land for white settlers.

Of far greater concern to the U.S. Army than the woodland tribes were approximately 125,000 Plains Indians who lived in the path of white settlement. They belonged to about thirty tribes, each with its own language, beliefs, and cultural traditions. Having lived in the region for generations, they were deeply attached to their homelands and defended them against all intruders, Indians and non-Indians alike. When whites began claiming these lands for themselves, hostilities broke out. One of the most famous incidents occurred in 1862, when the Santee Sioux Indians staged an uprising against white settlers in eastern Minnesota. In 1866–67, Sioux, Cheyenne, and Arapaho warriors led by Oglala chief Red Cloud attacked army forts along the Bozeman Trail, an

A ledger drawing by Howling Wolf entitled Cheyenne Village Scene: Treaty of Medicine Lodge *depicts treaty negotiations that established reservations for southern Cheyennes, Arapahoes, Kiowas, Comanches, and Apaches. To assist their efforts, U.S. officials often presented Indians with gifts like this pipe tomahawk.*

important settlers' route that cut through Indian lands in the Wyoming and Montana territories.

To resolve the "Indian problem," the federal government established a Peace Commission in 1867. Led by Nathan G. Taylor, head of the Office of Indian Affairs, and William T. Sherman, commanding general of the U.S. Army, the Peace Commission negotiated a series of important treaties with Plains tribes that ceded vast tracts of tribal territories in exchange for annuities and reservations. The Medicine Lodge Creek treaties, signed in 1867, defined two large reservations in western Indian Territory, one for Kiowas, Comanches, and Apaches and another for southern Cheyennes and Arapahoes. The Fort Laramie treaties, signed in 1868, established reservations in the Dakota Territory for northern Arapahoes, Crows, northern Cheyennes, and several Sioux bands.[1]

Together, these treaties cleared a broad swath of land for the Union Pacific Railroad, then under construction in central Nebraska, and for the thousands of white settlers following in its path. To separate Indians and whites, the treaties restricted reservations for the "absolute and undisturbed use and occupation of the tribes." The treaties also maintained the tribes' legal status as "domestic dependent nations" (so ruled by Chief Justice John Marshall in *Cherokee Nation v. Georgia* 1831) with their own governing authority. At the same time, however, the government placed all reservations under federal control and outlined plans to "civilize" Indians by providing them with physicians, schoolhouses, teachers, agricultural tools, and instructions on farming.[2]

Although the treaties declared peace, the situation on the Great Plains remained tense. When Ulysses S. Grant ran for president in 1868, he campaigned on the slogan "Let Us Have Peace," an olive branch extended to the Plains Indians as well as the former Confederacy. Developed during the period of Reconstruction, when war-weary Americans sought peace, Grant's Indian policy called for a harmonious approach between civilian, church, and military authorities. Christian missionaries, government agents, and army officers detailed to the Office of Indian Affairs would manage the reservations and "civilize" Indians, while the military would forcibly return any Indians found living off reservations. As described by Sherman, Grant's policy involved a dual effort of "peace within" and "war without."

Ironically, Grant's peace policy resulted in ten more years of warfare. While Pawnees, Hidatsas, Omahas, Blackfeet, and Crows never took up arms against the United States, others including the Sioux, Cheyennes, Arapahoes, Kiowas, and Comanches frequently did so. Most of the fighting occurred within the Division of the Missouri, commanded from Chicago by Lt. Gen. Philip H. Sheridan. A Civil War hero, Sheridan planned all major campaigns. With Sherman, he developed a strategy of total war, which meant attacking not only warriors on the battlefield, but entire villages where warriors lived with their families. Total war also called for the destruction of Indian property, including horses. This strategy not only destroyed Indians'

Although Ulysses S. Grant's 1868 presidential campaign promised peace, it delivered war to Plains Indians who refused to comply with the government's reservation program. U.S. Army officers who carried out Grant's policies included: Lt. Gen. Philip H. Sheridan (seated, second from left) with Lt. Col. George Armstrong Custer, Maj. Nelson B. Sweitzer, Lt. Col. James W. Forsyth and (standing left to right) Lt. Col. George A. Forsyth, Maj. Morris J. Asch, and Lt. Col. Michael V. Sheridan.

Opposite: As illustrated by this map of the Military Division of the Missouri, several railroad lines connected Chicago to the western front. Above: Troops Amassed against a Cheyenne Village, *a ledger drawing by Bear's Heart, 1876–77, conveys the horrors of total war as practiced by the U.S. Army during the Indian Campaigns.*

ability to wage war, but also their ability to hunt for food, thereby undermining their will to resist Army efforts to force them onto reservations. While acknowledging that tribes were often divided into "hostile" and "friendly" factions, both Sheridan and Sherman believed the only way to defeat the enemy was to hit them hard. As Sherman explained: "The Indians require to be soundly whipped and the ringleaders in the present trouble hung, their ponies killed, and such destruction of their property as will make them very poor."[3]

Although Sherman described Indian warfare in brutally simple terms, its realities proved to be far more difficult. Experienced from years of inter-tribal warfare and honored by their people for bravery, Indian warriors fought with great skill and courage. Superb horsemen, they used traditional bows, arrows, clubs, and tomahawks along with modern rifles, which had been primarily acquired through trade with whites. With few exceptions, Indians conducted a hit-and-run style of warfare, in contrast to the Euro-American style that involved large armies facing one another in major battles. Intimately familiar with their homelands, Indian warriors typically staged surprise attacks against their enemies, then quickly disappeared into the vast landscape.[4]

The U.S. Army paled in comparison to its Civil War strength. Immediately after the war ended in 1865, Congress reduced the army's size from a million men to a force of fifty-four thousand. Further reductions between 1869 and 1874 thinned the ranks to twenty-five thousand enlisted men, while discharge, death, and desertion continuously reduced the ranks. Most enlistees did not receive adequate training before reaching the front. They earned between thirteen and twenty-two dollars per month, slightly less than the wage of a common laborer. Reflecting an increasingly diverse population, the Army included a large number of Irish and German immigrants seeking a foothold in American society. Many African Americans (mostly former slaves) served in the Ninth and Tenth Cavalry and in the Twenty-fourth and Twenty-fifth Infantry. They became known as "Buffalo Soldiers."[5]

Although mediocrity characterized most officers, some young, ambitious men, such as Nelson A. Miles, provided strong leadership. Moreover, American troops had a slight edge over Indian warriors in terms of weaponry. Although Indians had acquired modern rifles as trade items or captured them in battle, they did not have ready supplies of ammunition or spare parts for repair. But more than any other factor, Sheridan and Sherman's strategy of total war proved to be the Army's most effective weapon.

Sheridan's troops first employed the tactics of total war against the Piegan Indians. On January 23, 1870, Maj. Eugene M. Baker led a squadron of cavalry against a Piegan village on Montana's Marias River. Baker's troops destroyed 44 lodges and killed 173 people, including 53 women and children, many suffering from smallpox. They also captured 140 women and children and more than 300 horses. Although Sheridan and Sherman defended Baker's actions by claiming Piegans had violated their treaty, the Piegan Massacre, as it became known, set off a storm of public protest that prompted Congress to prohibit the use of army officers as reservation agents. In addition, a measure to transfer the Office of Indian Affairs to the War Department failed to pass.[6]

Despite the controversy, Sheridan pursued total war in the Red River War, his first major campaign as division commander. Although it officially began in 1874, the Red River War actually continued the Southern Plains War of 1868–69, in which Kiowas, Comanches, Arapahoes, and Cheyennes resisted the terms of the Medicine Lodge Creek treaties. At that time, Sheridan commanded the Division of the Missouri and directed the Army's harsh

Col. Nelson A. Miles (above) and Col. Ranald S. Mackenzie (below) carried out a harsh campaign of total war in the Red River War of 1874–75. Both men later served in the Sioux War of 1876–77.

During the Red River War, Lone Wolf (left), and Satanta (right), led approximately twelve hundred Kiowa, Cheyenne, and Comanche warriors against the U.S. Army.

campaign that included the Battle of the Washita, in which the Seventh Cavalry, led by Lt. Col. George A. Custer, destroyed the village of Black Kettle, a prominent Cheyenne peace chief. Sheridan's efforts ultimately resulted in the confinement and concentration of the southern Plains tribes to the reservation, but the situation remained tense.

The restraints of reservation life, inadequate rations, and the wanton destruction of the Southern Plains buffalo herds by white hunters in 1872–73 put enormous pressures on the Indians. As had been their custom, Kiowa and Comanche warriors continued to raid frontier settlements from the Texas Panhandle to the Rio Grande River and by 1874, Cheyenne warriors had joined them. In response, Sheridan mounted an all-out attack. His plans closely followed that of the 1868–69 campaign by ordering several thousand troops from different directions to converge on the Staked Plains in the Texas Panhandle. About forty-eight hundred Kiowas, Comanches, and Cheyennes had fled to this desolate region where several forks of the Red River and deep canyons provided

ample cover. Although their numbers included an estimated twelve hundred mounted warriors, the rest were women, children, and elderly men.[7]

Col. Nelson A. Miles, Col. Ranald S. Mackenzie, and Lt. Col. George P. Buell commanded American forces against Kiowas led by Satanta and Lone Wolf, Cheyennes led by Grey Beard and Stone Calf, and Comanches led by Quanah Parker. Throughout the war, the opponents skirmished more than a dozen times, but neither side did much killing. American forces, however, waged total war several times, notably on the morning of September 28, 1874, when Mackenzie's troops struck a combined village of Kiowa, Comanche, and Cheyenne Indians in Palo Duro Canyon. Mackenzie's men only killed three Indians, but they burned the hastily abandoned camps, destroying all of their contents. To cripple Indian mobility, American forces seized 1,424 Indian horses and slaughtered all but 376. In similar actions, Buell's troops burned more than five hundred lodges in two abandoned villages, while Miles's forces destroyed a Cheyenne village of one hundred lodges.[8]

Chicago Missionaries

During the 1870s, Chicago's Woman's Board of Missions of the Interior (W.B.M.I.) supported Christian missionaries working among Sioux Indians. Jointly sponsored by the Congregational and Presbyterian churches, the W.B.M.I. had as its officers the socially prominent Sarah Seymour (Mrs. William) Blair and Mary Williams (Mrs. Eliphalet Wickes) Blatchford.

Like other missionary societies of the time, the W.M.B.I. believed that it had an obligation to teach American Indians the ways of white people so they could become "civilized" and, eventually, citizens of the United States. W.M.B.I. missionaries were dispatched to numerous locations, including Fort Sully, in Dakota Territory.

Fort Sully's educational program included a day school taught by Mary Collins, an evening school for young men taught by Emma Whipple, and three morning schools taught by native teachers. Lizzie Bishop and Louise M. Irive also served as missionary teachers. Between thirty and forty students attended each school, studying English, geography, and the Bible. Sewing classes also proved popular with the women, according to Mary Collins's accounts. In addition, with the help of Elisabeth, an American Indian teacher, Collins held a women's prayer meeting on Sunday that filled the prayer house to "overflowing, and more would have come had there been room." Collins's reports of the work at Fort Sully were enthusiastic, but Indian missionary work generally remained a haphazard effort for much of the late nineteenth century, with inadequately trained staff and limited resources.

Eighth Annual Report, Woman's Board of Missions of the Interior (Chicago: Culver, Page, Hoyne & Co., 1876), 17–18.

Ninth Annual Report, Woman's Board of Missions of the Interior (Chicago: Culver, Page, Hoyne & Co., 1876), 19–20.

Mary Collins, seated far right, with other missionaries and school children at Ft. Sully, South Dakota, 1883.

Lt. Col. George A. Custer's expedition to the Black Hills in 1874 opened the area for white settlement, but created conflict with Sioux Indians who, according to the terms of the Fort Laramie Treaty of 1868, had exclusive rights to the area.

Military pressures, severe weather conditions, and a lack of food forced a small number of Indians to surrender as early as October 1874, including Satanta. During the harsh winter, hundreds of Kiowas and Cheyennes surrendered, followed by Comanches in the spring. The mass surrenders not only signaled the end of the Red River War, but the end of all armed Indian resistance on the southern plains. Never again would Kiowa, Southern Cheyenne, or Comanche warriors oppose American forces on the battlefield.

For Sheridan, the Red River War validated the strategy of total war, and he used it again on the northern plains in 1876–77. Like the Red River War, the Sioux War resulted from a complex set of factors.[9] According to the terms of the 1868 Fort Laramie treaties establishing the Great Sioux Reservation west of the Missouri River, the Sioux retained hunting rights in the "unceded Indian ter-

ritory," a large area north of the North Platte River and east of the Big Horn Mountains. No white person could enter this territory without Sioux consent. During the early 1870s, several thousand Sioux lived in this area, led by young chiefs including Sitting Bull, Gall, Rain In The Face, and Crazy Horse. They hunted abundant game, raided enemy tribes, and defended the territory against white encroachment. When surveyors for the Northern Pacific Railroad plotted an extension along the Yellowstone River in the summer of 1873, Sioux warriors attacked its military escort, including troops of Custer's Seventh Cavalry.

The Black Hills became even more bitterly contested. By treaty, the verdant Black Hills, rich in game and fish, belonged to the Sioux, who considered them sacred ground, home of their gods and ancestors. But Sheridan wanted to establish a military presence, and in the summer of 1874, he sent Custer to the Black Hills with more than one thousand soldiers. Two miners who accompanied the expedition found enough traces of gold to whip up a gold fever across the country, then suffering from the Panic of 1873. By the summer of 1875, more than eight hundred gold miners hoping to "strike it rich" were working the streams of the Black Hills. Pressured by white settlers, who also demanded access, the government tried but failed to purchase the Black Hills from the Sioux for $6 million.

Gen. George F. Crook (left) and his forces took a beating at the Battle of the Rosebud on June 17, 1876. Eight days later, George A. Custer (above) and the Seventh Cavalry met their demise at the Battle of the Little Bighorn.

By late fall of 1875, the northern plains had become a powder keg, prompting the Office of Indian Affairs in December to order all Sioux living in the unceded territories to move onto their reservation by the end of January. When they failed to do so, the Army took action. Although Sheridan made plans to attack in the winter, when Indians remained in their villages, severe weather crippled troop movement. In the spring, nearly twenty-three hundred men under the command of Gen. Alfred A. Terry, Gen. George F. Crook, and Col. John A. Gibbon converged on the Sioux, then occupying lands south of the Yellowstone River in southeastern Montana. Despite the Army's large number of forces and proven strategy of convergence, Sheridan's campaign failed. On June 17, 1876, Sioux and

Cheyenne warriors led by Crazy Horse defeated Crook's forces at the Battle of the Rosebud. Eight days later, on June 25, Sioux, Cheyenne, and Arapaho warriors led by Gall, Crazy Horse, Two Moons, and other warrior chiefs annihilated Custer's Seventh Cavalry at the Battle of the Little Bighorn, killing 268 American soldiers.

Custer's defeat shocked the nation, then celebrating its centennial anniversary. "Horrible!" screamed the headlines of the *Chicago Tribune*, "The American Indian Exalts His Reputation for Satanic Ferocity." Custer's defeat, however, ultimately abetted the Army's effort to conquer the Sioux. In the wake of the disaster, Congress promptly approved a long-standing request from Sheridan and Sherman to build two new forts on tributaries of the Yellowstone River and authorized the enlistment of twenty-five hundred more men. Furthermore, the Army placed all Sioux agencies under its control and Sheridan ordered

Although Sitting Bull (above) was present at the Battle of the Little Bighorn, he did not participate in the fighting. Instead several other warriors, including Gall (right) and Rain In The Face (below) led the massive attack against Custer's forces.

several thousand troops to fan across Sioux territory and hound the enemy into unconditional surrender.

During the fall and winter of 1876–77, troops led by Crook, Mackenzie, and Miles carried out Sheridan's new plan of "total war." Mackenzie's troops attacked a Cheyenne village, destroying two hundred lodges, capturing seven hundred horses, and killing thirty warriors. Miles's foot soldiers pursued Sitting Bull and his followers across Montana throughout the fall, finally driving them into Canada. At the Battle of Wolf Mountain on January 8, 1877, Miles's troops forced Crazy Horse and his followers from the field.

That spring, nearly five thousand Indians, bowing to military pressures and peace terms negotiated by the Brulé Sioux leader, Spotted Tail, came into the agencies to surrender. After Miles's forces killed Lame Deer and fourteen Sioux warriors at the Battle of Muddy Creek on May 7, 1877, they burned Lame Deer's village and slaughtered more than two hundred Indian horses. For the next several months, Miles's soldiers pursued some two hundred followers of Lame Deer, hounding the last to surrender in September of 1877. By the end of the campaign, Miles's troops had marched more than four thousand miles and captured sixteen hundred horses, ponies, and mules.

They had killed, captured, forced to surrender, or driven out of the territory about seven thousand Indians. Only Sitting Bull and his followers remained free, living in Canada until they finally surrendered in 1881.[10]

Although there were additional conflicts with Nez Perce, Ute, and Northern Cheyenne Indians, the conclusion of the Sioux War put an end to serious Indian resistance on the Great Plains. Essentially, the military had accomplished its mission of forcibly moving all Plains Indians to reservations, allowing Sheridan to comment in his January 1879 report to Congress: "There has been no general combination of hostile Indians in this military division during the past year, and I doubt that such conditions can exist again." Since 1869, Sheridan's forces had been in nearly four hundred skirmishes, combats, and battles with Plains Indians. More than one thousand officers and enlisted men were killed or wounded in these encounters. After 1879, the army spent most of its time keeping Indians contained on reservations rather than pursuing them across the frontier.[11]

Despite the army's hard-won victories, the government still had an "Indian problem," largely of its own making. Underfunded and poorly administered, federal reservations held the vast majority of Indians in squalid conditions, subject to hunger, epidemic disease, and high death rates. Further appalled by a growing financial scandal involving the Office of Indian Affairs, critics across the country demanded reform. Led by the Boston Indian Citizenship Committee, the Women's National Indian Association and the Indian Rights Association, reformers insisted that Indians should be completely assimilated into the American mainstream instead of being isolated on reservations. Toward that end, reformers argued for breaking up reservations, where tribes held land in common, into individual plots of land. By dividing up tribal lands, reformers argued, allotment would break down Indians' cultural identities so that they could become more like white people. Allotment would also make Indians private property owners and farmers who would become economically independent and eventually, American citizens with equal rights before the law.[12]

Many Americans, who once believed in the complete separation of Indians and whites, now found themselves agreeing with the reformers. Reservations not only kept Indians in a "backward state," they also tied up vast amounts of land coveted by white settlers and business interests. For Congress, the scandal-ridden Office of Indian Affairs had become a political embarrassment, and the Army had grown tired of policing reservations. Everyone, it seemed, wanted change. From the white perspective, however, that required a fundamental change on the part of Indians. They could no longer remain tribal people, but must enter the modern age. As stated by the *Chicago Tribune*, "If he [the Indian] would become 'civilized,' he must either till the soil or embark in mechanics, the arts, or literature."[13]

During the 1880s, Sen. Henry L. Dawes of Massachusetts took up the cause of assimilation. His efforts culminated in 1887 with the passage of the General Allotment Act. Under its terms, each Indian head of family could receive a patent for 160 acres of land to be held in trust by the United States government for twenty-five years; citizenship in the state or territory of residence accompanied the patent. When all Indians on a particular reservation accepted allotments, or sooner if the President decided, the U.S. could negotiate with the tribe for its surplus lands, which would then be opened to settlement under the Homestead Act.

Hailed by reformers as the dawn of a new age in Indian relations, allotment wreaked havoc on reservations by providing the legal means to reduce their size. Between 1887 and 1934, when allotment stopped, Indians lost nearly ninety million acres of tribal lands. In addition to the loss of land, allotment eroded tribal authority and weakened cultural traditions among people spiritually tied to the land. Tragically, allotment further impoverished Indians because their small plots of land could not support farming or ranching, which in the West, requires large, contiguous blocks of land.[14]

Allotment led to the Sioux Act of 1889, which broke up the Great Sioux Reservation into six smaller reservations: Pine Ridge, Rosebud, Cheyenne River, Standing Rock, Crow Creek, and Lower Brulé. All of these reservations lay within the Division of the Missouri, now commanded by Gen. Nelson Miles. Understandably, poverty, deadly epidemics of smallpox and cholera, and the loss of their homelands led many Sioux to seek relief in the Ghost Dance, a new religious movement among western tribes.

POCKET MAP

Gift from
Howard Miller

BENNETT COUNTY
SOUTH DAKOTA

INCLUDING THAT PART OF THE

PINE RIDGE INDIAN RESERVATION

SOON TO BE OPENED FOR

Free Homestead Settlement

PUBLISHED BY

CHARLES A. BATES
LACREEK
SOUTH DAKOTA

Map of BENNETT COUNTY, SOUTH DAKOTA, Compiled under the supervision of Chas. Ash Bates, U

*The General Allotment Act of 1887 authorized
the division of tribal lands into separate parcels
for individual owners. On Pine Ridge Indian
Reservation in South Dakota, allotment began
in the early 1900s, with government surveyors
using allotment stakes to mark boundary lines
at one-mile increments. As noted by the
pamphlet, unassigned lands were opened
to homesteaders, predominantly whites.*

Short Bull (left) and Kicking Bear, leaders of the Ghost Dance Movement among Sioux Indians.

Originating with Wovoka, a Paiute shaman, the Ghost Dance predicted the coming of a peaceful world in which Indians would be reunited with dead friends and relatives for all eternity. Among the Sioux, Ghost Dance leaders Kicking Bear and Short Bull foretold of the day when whites would disappear from the earth, leaving Indians again free to practice their beliefs and customs.[15]

Fearing the Ghost Dance would lead to an uprising on the Pine Ridge and Rosebud reservations, the government sent in six hundred armed forces under the command of Brig. Gen. John R. Brooke in November of 1890. Meanwhile, in Chicago, Miles ordered the arrest of Sitting Bull, who had been living at Standing Rock since his return from Canada in 1881. Sitting Bull still commanded a loyal following among his people and encouraged the Ghost Dance. When Indian policemen tried to arrest him in his cabin on the morning of December 15,

1890, a fight broke out and police shot and killed the legendary chief. Six policemen and several of Sitting Bull's followers also died. The death of Sitting Bull, the greatest figure of Indian resistance, sent four hundred Hunkpapa Sioux from Standing Rock fleeing toward the Cheyenne River reservation and Big Foot, a Ghost Dance leader whose arrest Miles also sought.

Although stricken with pneumonia, Big Foot led about 350 followers, including more than 200 women and children, toward Pine Ridge. On December 28, four troops of the Seventh Cavalry intercepted Big Foot's people, convinced them to accept a military escort, and camped with them that evening at Wounded Knee. The next morning, five hundred soldiers surrounded the Indians. Acting on orders from General Brooke, Col. James W. Forsyth demanded that the Indians surrender their guns. When Big Foot's followers refused to comply, the soldiers searched the tents. Tensions mounted and, when two soldiers and an Indian began to scuffle, a gun went off. All hell broke loose as soldiers and Indians fought hand-to-hand, using guns, swords, and clubs. Women and children fled in terror. When the hand-to-hand fighting abruptly stopped, the artillery, positioned on an adjoining hilltop, opened fire with Hotchkiss cannons, leveling the village, and cutting down fleeing groups of Indians with deadly rounds of ammunition. When the shooting ended, more than 150 Indians lay dead. They included Big Foot plus eighty-three men and boys, forty-four women, and eighteen children. Another fifty Indians lay wounded. Twenty-five Army officers and soldiers died, while thirty-nine had been wounded.

When Miles learned of the events at Wounded Knee, he immediately relieved Forsyth of his command and ordered an investigation. Although Miles believed that some "hostile" Indians still posed a military threat, he considered Forsyth's actions an outrageous blunder. And despite the carnage, Short Bull's and Kicking Bear's followers still remained at large. Taking matters into his own hands, Miles traveled to Pine Ridge and surrounded the Indian village with thirty-five hundred soldiers at a considerable distance. Another two thousand soldiers stood by at a still greater distance. Over the next several days, Miles slowly moved his circle of troops closer and closer to the village, all the while making peace overtures. Gradually, the

Indians began to surrender and on January 15, 1891, with no further bloodshed, Miles ended the crisis.[16]

With its threat of becoming a new "Indian War," Wounded Knee had become a national media event. In the fall, several photographers and more than two dozen reporters had descended upon Pine Ridge. The presence of William F. "Buffalo Bill" Cody and his manager, Maj. John M. Burke, added to the circus-like atmosphere. Chicago reporter Gilbert E. Bailey of the *Inter Ocean* reported from Pine Ridge in typical yellow-journalism style with sensational headlines and lurid descriptions of Indians as "sav-

ages," "hostiles," "redskins," and "half-breeds." While Bailey's illustrated reports provided readers with a considerable amount of information, his bias undoubtedly convinced readers that the events at Wounded Knee constituted a "battle" rather than a terrible tragedy.[17]

On the evening of January 27, 1891, Miles returned to Chicago with forty-one Sioux Indians from Pine Ridge. According to the *Inter Ocean*, a large crowd of "curious folk who wanted to see the survivors of the latest American war" met them at the Chicago & North Western Railway depot. Although the crowd nearly blocked the

When the shooting stopped at Wounded Knee, more than 150 Sioux Indians, including many women and children lay dead. A national media event, Wounded Knee attracted dozens of journalists and photographers, who sensationalized the tragedy as a "battle."

Above: Upon learning of the tragic events, Gen. Nelson A. Miles traveled to Wounded Knee from his Chicago headquarters and ended the conflict without further bloodshed. Afterward, he took twenty-seven Ghost Dancers to Chicago and imprisoned them at Fort Sheridan (below). Kicking Bear and Short Bull are identified on the photograph as numbers four and five, respectively.

tracks and clamored for the Indians to stage a pow-wow or Ghost Dance, Miles remained firmly in control. He hurried seventeen Indians who had helped negotiate the settlement at Pine Ridge to the Fort Wayne Railroad depot, where they boarded a train for Washington and a meeting with Thomas J. Morgan, Commissioner of Indian Affairs. Miles took the remaining Ghost Dancers to Fort Sheridan, thirty miles north of Chicago, where he imprisoned them.[18]

Fearing a Sioux uprising in the spring, Miles planned to keep the Ghost Dancers at Fort Sheridan for six months, but Buffalo Bill Cody had another idea. Owner of a phenomenally successful Wild West show, Cody never passed up an opportunity to increase ticket sales. Despite the fact that the government forbade the hiring of Indians for entertainment purposes, Cody, a former military scout, wielded his considerable influence and secured the release of the Ghost Dancers for a year-long tour of Europe.[19]

The Plains Indian Wars concluded with Wounded Knee, as did Chicago's position as military headquarters. In 1892, the army underwent a major reorganization, eliminating the Division of the Missouri in the process.
At last, after more than twenty years, peace had arrived, but the conflict became a bitter legacy for all Americans, as well as a sobering reminder that throughout history, great migrations and nation-building have caused conflict and war.

NOTES FOR CHAPTER THREE: WAR WITHOUT

1. Charles J. Kappler, ed., *Indian Treaties 1778–1883* (Mattiluck, New York: Amereon House), 977–89, 998–1015; Robert M. Utley, *The Indian Frontier of the American West, 1846–1890* (Albuquerque: University of New Mexico Press, 1984), 114–20.

2. Charles F. Wilkerson, *American Indians, Time and the Law* (New Haven: Yale University Press, 1987), 14–19.

3. Robert M. Utley, *Frontier Regulars: The United States Army and The Indian, 1866–1890* (New York: Macmillan Publishing Co., Inc., 1973), 149.

4. Ibid., 46–47.

5. Ibid., 17–23, 26–27.

6. Ibid., 198–99; Lt. Gen. P. H. Sheridan, *Record of Engagements with Hostile Indians within the Military Division of the Missouri from 1869 to 1882* (Chicago: Headquarters Military Division of the Missouri, 1882).

7. This summary of the Red River War is based upon Utley's account in *Frontier Regulars*, 225–39.

8. Ibid., 232–33; October 12, 1874 telegram received at Chicago Military Headquarters, Division of the Missouri.

9. This summary of the Sioux War is based upon Utley's account in *Frontier Regulars*, 243–69.

10. Sheridan, *Record of Engagements*, 84.

11. Paul Andrew Hutton, *Phil Sheridan and His Army* (Lincoln, Nebraska: University of Nebraska Press, 1985), 331.

12. Frederick E. Hoxie, *A Final Promise: The Campaign to Assimilate the Indians, 1880–1920* (New York: Cambridge University Press, 1995), 1–15.

13. *Chicago Tribune*, October 21, 1879.

14. Wilkerson, *American Indians*, 20.

15. This summary of Wounded Knee is based upon the account in Richard E. Jensen, R. Eli Paul, and John E. Carter, *Eyewitness at Wounded Knee* (Lincoln, Nebraska: University of Nebraska Press, 1991), 3–6, and Utley, *Frontier Regulars*, 407–21.

16. Utley, *Frontier Regulars*, 419.

17. *The Daily Inter Ocean*, December 4, 1890 to January 18, 1891.

18. *The Daily Inter Ocean*, January 29, 1891; Jensen et al., *Eyewitness*, 171.

19. Jensen et al., *Eyewitness*, 171.

A photograph taken around 1890 of a western farm family standing next to a McCormick harvester illustrates one aspect of Chicago's economic empire.

FOUR

An Economic Empire

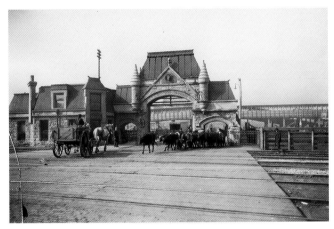

Views of the Union Stock Yards, c. 1880, illustrate its arched entrance on Union Street (above) and a sea of animal pens that covered forty acres (below). Several major railroad lines linked the Yards to the rich cattle lands of the West.

Western expansion fueled Chicago's spectacular growth during the late nineteenth century. As the West became more settled, its farmers and ranchers sent grain and livestock to the city, while the city returned a staggering array of supplies and consumer goods. As a result, Chicago became the chief marketplace of the West, as well as its economic capital. Although several cities like Minneapolis, St. Paul, and St. Louis developed ties to western markets, none surpassed Chicago, which, by 1890, became the nation's second largest city (behind New York).

Trade between Chicago and the West was facilitated by the railroads. In addition to passengers, they hauled millions of tons of freight, generating millions of dollars in profits. After the Civil War, a large percentage of this freight came into and out of Chicago's Union Stock Yards. Incorporated and financed with more than $1 million by nine railroads, including the Chicago, Burlington & Quincy, the Chicago & North Western, and the Chicago, Rock Island & Pacific, the stockyards officially opened for business on Christmas Day in 1865. The Yards, as they became known, consolidated several stock enclosures, scattered across the city, into one large area on the southwest side, just outside the city limits.[1]

To help create a modern facility, the railroads hired Octave Chanute, a civil engineer formerly employed by the Chicago & Alton Railroad. Plotted on 160 acres of land, Chanute's plans included fifteen miles of railroad track and five hundred animal pens on forty acres. Thirty miles of sewers effectively drained the low-lying, swampy area, and modern pumps delivered five hundred thousand gallons of water each day from the west branch of the Chicago River's South Fork. Two main thoroughfares, seventy-five and sixty-six feet wide respectively, provided drovers with ample space to herd their animals from the trains to the pens.

With its ample accommodations, including a six-story hotel and a commodious office building, the Yards exceeded everyone's expectations. Between 1865 and 1870, its receipts jumped from $1.5 million to more than $3 million with an annual profit of $150,000.[2]

Forty-six meatpacking companies surrounded the Yards and they, too, used modern technology to increase production. During the 1860s, overhead steel rails and trolleys replaced wooden ones, making the moving of butchered animal carcasses easier and faster. Another modern device, the steam-powered pig-hoist, raised the live hog by its hind leg and attached it to the elevated rail, allowing workers to kill, scald, scrape, and gut the suspended animal in a matter of minutes. Ice-cooled refrigerator units preserved freshly butchered meat, thereby extending the packing season from the cold-weather months into the spring and summer. Gustavus Swift developed the first refrigerated railroad car in 1882, making possible the shipping of fresh meat over long distances.

Above: Views in the Chicago Stock Yards, *published in 1892, provided an inside look at the slaughter houses.* Below: *The refrigerated railroad car, developed by Gustavus Swift in 1882, allowed for the shipment of fresh meat from Chicago to distant markets.*

During the late 1800s, Chicago became the meat-processing capital of the world. Trimming knives, a meat cleaver, and a cast iron bull's head from the Stockyards Inn are some of the few materials that remain from an industry that once dominated the city's economy.

During the 1870s Indian Campaigns, the U.S. Army employed hundreds of scouts to track the enemy. Although scouts didn't have official uniforms, this buckskin outfit, c. 1875, is typical of what many of them wore. The army also employed many American Indian scouts from tribes considered "friendly," such as the Crow Indians. Above: A Cheyenne ledger drawing, White Scout, c. 1880.

For generations, Sioux Indians created visual records of the past known as "winter counts." Each image represents an important event for a particular year. This example from Standing Rock Reservation spans the years 1798–1919. Below: A finely beaded, papoose toy and child's vest made by Sioux Indians during the reservation period, c. 1890.

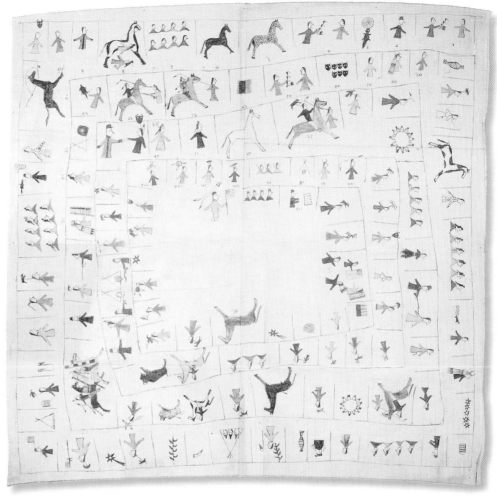

The McCormick Company of Chicago excelled at advertising that incorporated popular myth with romantic imagery. "The maiden reaper" symbolized the virtues of living in rural America (left). One of the company's lithographs (below) presents western expansion as a glorious epic, led by none other than McCormick reapers! Although the advertisement distorts reality, it alludes to the fact that, during the late 1800s, the West became one of McCormick's most important markets.

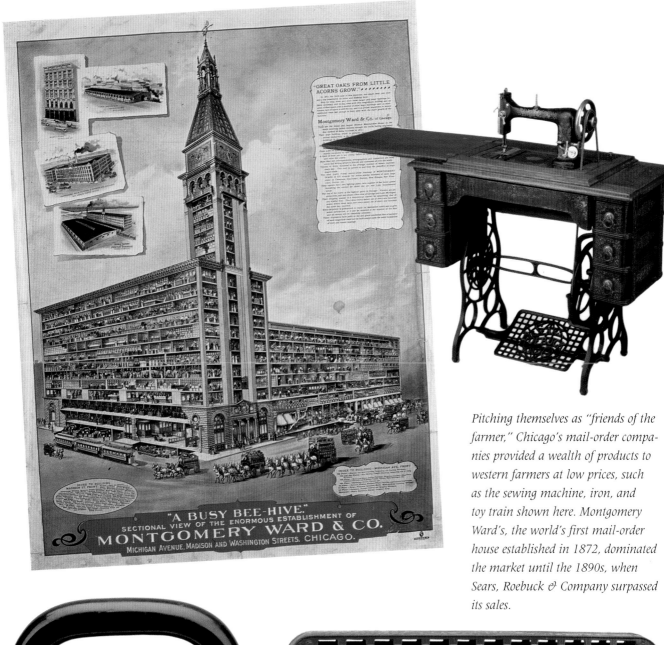

Pitching themselves as "friends of the farmer," Chicago's mail-order companies provided a wealth of products to western farmers at low prices, such as the sewing machine, iron, and toy train shown here. Montgomery Ward's, the world's first mail-order house established in 1872, dominated the market until the 1890s, when Sears, Roebuck & Company surpassed its sales.

After the Civil War, the Schuttler Wagon Company of Chicago became the leading manufacturer of grain wagons used in the West. Farmers typically used these wagons to haul grain from their fields to local markets and railroad warehouses.

William F. "Buffalo Bill" Cody's Wild West Show provided a spectacular view of the past, with little attention to historical accuracy. At the 1893 Columbian Exposition in Chicago, Cody's colorful troupe of performers outdrew many other attractions.

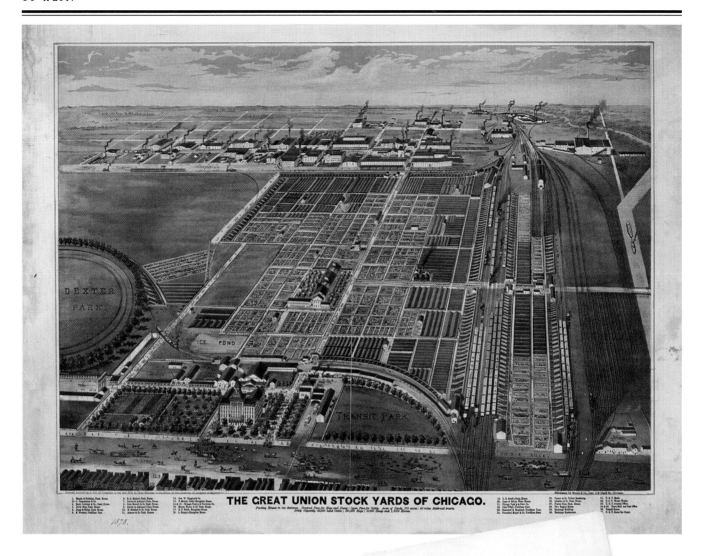

THE GREAT UNION STOCK YARDS OF CHICAGO.

A bird's-eye view of Chicago's Union Stock Yards in 1878 not only captures its grand size, but clearly illustrates its proximity to the railroads. Surrounding the Yards were dozens of processing plants, including the Cudahy Meatpacking Company, whose 1890s pamphlet, From the Ranch to the Table *(below)* explained the close relationship between western cattle ranches and Chicago's meatpacking industry.

By 1890, Chicago's meatpacking industry, dominated by the Swift, Armour, Morris, Hammond, and Cudahy companies, employed more than seventeen thousand people, making it the largest employer in the city. Together they produced 82 percent of all meat consumed in United States.[3]

Cattle ranching, the western half of Chicago's giant livestock and meatpacking industries, also became a modern business in the late nineteenth century. Before the Civil War, the raising of western cattle had been a small industry, primarily located in Texas, but after the war, it boomed with the growth of western railroads. Texas cattlemen, whose animals were banned from markets in Missouri and Kansas because they carried a deadly fever, began to drive huge cattle herds of two to three thousand head up the legendary Chisholm, Western, and Goodnight-Loving trails to the Kansas and Union Pacific Railroads in central Kansas and southern Nebraska. Towns like Abilene, Wichita, Dodge City, and Ogallala sprang up overnight. Drovers soon discovered that cattle held on the northern ranges in cold weather did not succumb to the fever. (It was later learned that ticks caused the fever and were killed by the cold weather.) These cattle could now be shipped safely to Kansas City, St. Louis, and most importantly, to the Union Stock Yards in Chicago. As a result, business boomed; from thirty-five thousand cattle coming up the Chisholm Trail in 1865, approximately six hundred thousand came four years later.

In a pattern typical of the post–Civil War economy, the cattle boom quickly collapsed. A surplus of animals, the harsh winter of 1871–72, and the Panic of 1873 dealt a serious blow to the industry from which it didn't begin to recover until the late 1870s. By then, western cattlemen faced a new set of circumstances. As the West became more settled, the open range disappeared. Wealthy eastern and foreign investors began to take over the industry. Between 1882 and 1886, British and American investors sunk hundreds of millions of dollars in western ranches, establishing hundreds of companies in Wyoming, New Mexico, Montana, and Colorado.

Several Chicago businessmen, including retailer Marshall Field and meatpacker Nelson Morris, along with dry goods merchants John V. and Charles B. Farwell, invested in western ranching. As controlling members of an American and British syndicate, the Farwells owned the world's largest cattle ranch—the three-million-acre XIT Ranch in the Texas Panhandle. Along with Chicago businessmen Abner Taylor and Amos C. Babcock, the Farwells established the XIT in 1885 on lands they received as payment from the cash-strapped state of Texas for constructing a new state capitol in Austin.[4]

XIT's managing director, John Farwell, organized the ranch into eight divisions, each with its own headquarters, foreman, and group of cowboys. He instituted strict accounting methods, requiring his foremen to submit monthly reports on payroll and the condition of the cattle, range, and water. Ranch foremen also noted cattle births, deaths, and sales and kept a daily record of the weather. At considerable cost, Farwell had the ranch

John V. Farwell (above), a wealthy Chicago businessman, was a controlling partner of a syndicate that owned the huge XIT Ranch in the Texas Panhandle. As its manager, Farwell instituted modern practices on the ranch.

The largest cattle ranch in the world, the XIT covered three million acres, had 150,000 head of cattle, and employed more than one hundred cowboys. Above: When he visited the XIT Ranch, John Farwell held Sunday religious services for the cowboys, as in this 1898 photograph. Below: Texas longhorn hat rack, c. 1900. Bottom: XIT cowboys branding cattle, c. 1900.

fenced with six thousand miles of barbed wire, erected more than three hundred windmills, and installed one of the first telephone lines in the Texas Panhandle at the ranch headquarters. Like other modern cattlemen, Farwell increased and improved his longhorn herd through selective breeding with eastern shorthorn Herefords and Durhams to produce a much more flavorful product. By the early 1900s, the XIT herd numbered 150,000 head and its quality helped raise livestock standards throughout Texas.[5]

Each year, the XIT employed about 120 cowboys. Most of them were young, single, and white. They earned about thirty dollars per month, plus meals and a horse, but had to furnish their own clothing, bedding, saddle, and tack. XIT cowboys also had to abide by a strict set of rules against card playing, gambling, drinking, and entertaining disreputable people—defined as loafers, deadbeats, tramps, or gamblers—at any of the camps. Like other big ranches, the XIT insisted upon well-behaved employees who wouldn't cause trouble.[6]

Preoccupied with many responsibilities in Chicago, Farwell managed the XIT from afar, rarely visiting the ranch more than once a year. Despite Farwell's business acumen, the XIT consistently lost money, and the XIT syndicate began to sell its land to pay off its investors in 1900. John Farwell oversaw the sales and continued to manage the ranch until 1905, three years before his death. The XIT remained in operation until 1912; the Farwell heirs sold the last of its lands in 1963.[7]

John Clay, a livestock commissioner originally from Scotland, helped modernize the cattle business in ways similar to Farwell's. After coming to Chicago in 1872, Clay began to buy and sell cattle for British interests, serving as a middleman between cattlemen and investors in a fast moving market. With dozens of other dealers, Clay worked out of the National Livestock Bank at the Union Stock Yards. In addition, Clay managed several western ranches. One of the largest was the Swan Ranch in Wyoming, which he purchased for British investors after it had failed in 1887, the result of mismanagement and the great "die up" of western cattle in the harsh winter of 1886. At the time, the ranch spread over half a million acres and had about 120,000 head of cattle. When Clay became manager in 1888, he introduced several new

John Clay, a livestock commissioner originally from Scotland, helped modernize the cattle business. Among other accomplishments, he established the International Livestock Exposition in Chicago.

business methods to save the ranch. As Clay observed, "the old system of open range was passing" and changes "had to come."[8]

To begin with, Clay rented the Swan's separate divisions to tenants who fenced in large pasturelands of hay for the feeding of cattle. He reorganized the company's finances, reduced the company's land holdings by 283,226 acres, and thinned the cattle herd to forty thousand head which required fewer cowboys. Like Farwell, Clay improved the ranch's herd by bringing in eastern purebred bulls to breed with selected females. "When it comes to building up a herd," Clay observed, "you can make much more progress in the female side than on the male. It is simply marvelous how quick a breeding herd responds to this class of management."[9]

INTERNATIONAL LIVE STOCK EXPOSITION

Official Catalog

International Amphitheatre

Union Stock Yards Chicago

NOVEMBER THE TWENTY-SEVENTH TO DECEMBER THE TENTH, NINETEEN HUNDRED AND NINE

Held every year in early December from 1900 to 1975, the International Livestock Exposition attracted animal breeders and dealers from across the country. Its official catalog always featured an image of the "Bronze Bull" trophy, awarded to winners of the collegiate division contest.

As a professional cattleman, Clay helped establish several organizations, including the Wyoming Stock Growers Association and the International Livestock Exposition in Chicago. The exposition succeeded the American Fat Stock, Horse, Poultry, and Dairy Shows, originally established as the Fat Stock Show in 1877 by the Illinois State Board of Agriculture. Held in the glass-domed Exposition Building on Michigan Avenue, these early shows served as important venues for breeders to showcase and market their animals. After the Exposition Building was demolished in 1891 for the construction of the Art Institute of Chicago, livestock breeders staged smaller contests elsewhere in the city, but they failed to convince the "business interests of this city which draw their life-blood from the farm" of the need for a larger show. Taking the initiative, Clay and several associates, including John A. Spoor of the Union Stock Yards, J. O. Armour, and Edward F. Swift, organized the International Livestock Exposition. Clay, Armour, and Swift sat on the executive board of the exposition, while Spoor served as president.[10]

Financed by the Union Stock Yard & Transit Company, the first International Livestock Exposition opened on December 1, 1900, at the Dexter Park Amphitheatre, a large, domed structure located next to the yards. The eight-day event attracted hundreds of entries and thousands of visitors. Livestock experts from across the country judged various classes of cattle, sheep, swine, and draft horses. In the cattle division, monetary prizes ranged from ten dollars for a fourth-place finish to one hundred dollars for the Grand Champion steer or heifer.[11]

The Farwells of the XIT Ranch awarded prizes from twenty-five to one hundred dollars for the best carload of steers bred in the Southwest District (Arizona, New Mexico, Oklahoma, and Texas). Not to be outclassed, John Clay sponsored an inter-collegiate stock judging contest for agricultural departments at midwestern and western colleges. The winner of the collegiate division took home the famous "Bronze Bull," otherwise known as the Spoor Trophy. Beginning in 1901, an image of the trophy appeared each year on the front cover of the catalog and became the official symbol of the exposition.[12]

As noted by Clay, the International Livestock Exposition brought the West to Chicago, where the city could "pay back" its vital trading partners with the latest information about raising cattle. Clay stated that, "Texas met Montana and California shook hands with New York. No one who was present will ever forget the extraordinary interest taken by the country visitors, and for the first time in our recollection the city people seemed to grasp the importance of the Exposition, and are now heart and soul with it." According to Clay, the exposition provided the city with the "first genuine outburst of agrarian loyalty to Chicago in the neighboring states." Aimed at big breeders, rather than small ranchers or farmers, the exposition became the nation's most important forum for sharing information on breeds and techniques of animal husbandry and remained in Chicago until 1975.[13]

Although the exposition and large ranches such as the XIT dominate the image most people have of cattle raising, they represent only part of the story. Even during the 1880s, when western cattle ranching reached its peak, big ranches accounted for only 14 percent of all slaughter beef produced in the United States. Small, diversified farmers accounted for the rest. Dubbed "nesters" by ranchers and cowboys who scoffed at their settled ways, western farmers practiced a mixed type of agriculture that included cash crops and livestock production. Using modern equipment like mechanical reapers, western farmers turned the fertile soils of the Great Plains into one of the most productive agricultural regions on earth.

More than any other machine, the reaper made western agriculture possible and profitable. Patented in 1832 by Cyrus H. McCormick of Virginia, the reaper consisted of paddles on a rotating wheel that pressed the grain against a vibrating, four-and-a-half-foot long blade, then pushed the cut stalks onto a platform. A laborer walking behind the reaper raked the stalks off the platform, bound them into sheaves, and stacked them in the fields to dry. Using a reaper, a farmer could harvest five to six acres of grain per day, compared to one acre per day with a hand-held sickle or scythe.

Sensing better opportunities in the West, McCormick moved to Chicago in 1847, opened a factory next to the Chicago River, and began to market his reaper to farmers in Illinois and Wisconsin. After his patent expired in 1848, McCormick faced stiff competition from numerous

As seen in an aerial view, c. 1910, the McCormick Works had easy access to the city's railroad network via its own spur lines. It was located on Blue Island and Western Avenues, near the Chicago River.

Established by Cyrus H. McCormick in 1847, the McCormick Works of Chicago made thousands of reapers and harvesters for western farmers. A view of the mower manufacturing room, c. 1910, illustrates how mechanization speeded up production.

McCormick advertisements always presented a rosy view of farm life. Happy wheat farmers in North Dakota (below) gave the "glad hand."

rivals such as D. M. Osborne and Gammon & Deering. A shrewd businessman, McCormick extended credit to cash-strapped farmers and aggressively promoted his products by placing large ads in newspapers and agricultural journals like the Chicago-based *Prairie Farmer.* His tactics paid off. From five hundred reapers sold in 1848, sales rose to about twenty-five hundred machines a year by 1855. During the Civil War, high prices, favorable weather, and increased demand from domestic and overseas markets stimulated grain production. Like its competitors, the McCormick Company prospered during the war, and by 1865 some 250,000 reapers and mowers were in use across the country.[14]

After the war, several McCormick competitors began producing a new type of machine known as the harvester. Originally developed in the early 1860s by the Marsh Brothers of Shabonna Grove, Illinois, the harvester took the basic function of the reaper one step further with a revolving apron of canvas or wooden slats that lifted the cut grain from the platform and deposited it on a table located on the rear platform. Two men seated at the table then bundled and tied the grain into sheaves, doing as much in a day as four workers following the self-rake reaper. While self-rake reapers continued to sell well in the East and Midwest, harvesters became very

popular among western farmers in the new wheat areas of Nebraska and Minnesota.

At first, McCormick considered the harvester a "humbug," but the demand from western farmers finally forced the company to begin manufacturing its own version in 1875. Over the next ten years, McCormick sold thousands of harvesters, later improved with automatic twine binders, to western farmers. The Red River Valley in western Minnesota became an especially good market. By the late 1870s, its farmers, blessed with several years of exceptionally good weather, were producing twenty to twenty-five bushels of wheat per acre, 50 percent more than the U.S. average, for a total of eight million bushels. Several hundred-thousand-acre "bonanza" farms, owned by individuals or syndicates, dominated the region's economy. By aggressively promoting its product and cutting prices, McCormick captured this market, claiming in 1880 that its machines cut half the wheat grown in the Red River Valley.[15]

During the 1880s, when the West grew at an unprecedented rate, the McCormick Company sold more machines than at any other time in its history. In 1883, the company sold forty-eight thousand machines that would, claimed the company, form a parade 273 miles long, "the grandest army of all the ages, and bound on the grandest mission—peace." The company's self-aggrandizing style of advertising reached a peak with advertisements like "Hurrah! The Farmers Give McCormick the Glad Hand," in which everyone appears to prosper under McCormick's influence.[16]

In truth, McCormick's machines did help farmers greatly increase production. Between 1860 and 1900, new technology such as mechanical harvesters, along with improvements in transportation, the growth of great urban markets, and an increased demand for exports raised the Gross Farm Product by 164 percent. The overall value of American farm lands, buildings, implements and machinery, work animals and livestock, and crop inventories rose 104 percent, compared to 24 percent for the years 1900–20. On the Great Plains, farm value increased by more than 1,000 percent.[17]

Yet, all was not well. Western farmers protested the high cost of transportation and the low prices paid for their products. To address farmers' concerns, Milton George of Chicago founded the Farmers' Alliance for Cook County, Illinois on April 15, 1880. George, a successful farmer from Fulton County in western Illinois, had moved to Chicago in 1871 to assume control of *The Western Rural*, a struggling farm journal in which he had invested. Under his direction, the weekly paper published lengthy editorials criticizing the railroads for exploiting farmers with high rates, and he urged farmers to defend themselves with transportation clubs and alliances such as the Granger organizations of the 1870s.[18]

A friend of the farmer, Milton George (above) fought for economic reform through political means. As editor of the Western Rural, *George used its pages as a mouthpiece of the Farmers' Alliance, a grass-roots organization that had strong support in the West.*

Through the Cook County Alliance, George established many branches throughout the country. Eventually, the organization became the National, or Northern, Farmers' Alliance. George described the Alliance as a political organization that "has for its object the relief of the producer from the extortions of monopoly, to secure equal taxation, to secure protection against the unjust assessment of the owners of patents and to prevent the adulteration of farm products which are now flooding the market. It simply demands and is laboring for freedom, right and justice for the farmer."[19]

On October 14, 1880, the Alliance attracted about five hundred members to Farwell Hall in Chicago for a farmers' transportation convention. The convention, representing "Grangers, Farmers' Clubs and Alliances," adopted lengthy resolutions condemning the railroads as a "virtual monopoly . . . oppressive alike to the producer and consumer, corrupting to our politics, a hindrance to free and impartial legislation, and a menace to the very safety of our republican institutions." To correct matters, the convention called upon the federal government to institute rate control.[20]

By 1882, the Alliance, headquartered in Chicago at 157 Dearborn Street, claimed a membership of one hundred thousand farmers enrolled in thousands of local alliances in Nebraska, Kansas, Iowa, Minnesota, Illinois, Wisconsin, Michigan, and Missouri. Early interest in the organization can be attributed to declining farm prices and a drought in the upper Midwest in 1881 that greatly reduced crop yields. When conditions improved in 1883–84, interest in the Alliance declined. Very few farmers attended the 1883 convention in Chicago, and the following year no meeting was held.

When high yields on the Great Plains forced wheat prices down in 1884–85, thousands of western farmers flocked back to the Alliance. The brutal winter of 1886–87 and several summer droughts forced tens of thousands of farmers and ranchers in Dakota, Kansas, and Nebraska into bankruptcy. "The Farmers' Alliance has never shown so much life as it is now showing," rejoiced George. "More alliances are being organized than ever before, especially in the West." When the Alliance held its national meeting in Minneapolis in October 1887, members called for more radical reforms.[21]

Led by George, the Alliance demanded the free coinage of silver that would put more money into farmers' hands, the removal of taxes from the necessities of life (defined as sugar, lumber, salt, coal, and clothing), and a graduated income tax to give "greatly needed relief to productive labor." The Alliance also called for reduced railroad rates; government ownership of one transcontinental railroad line; the direct election of U.S. senators; and the establishment of an educational system based on a "moral, manual and intellectual training that inculcates the essential dignity and necessity of honest labor."[22]

By 1890, the Northern Alliance had become a potent political force in the West. Orators like Ignatius Donnelly of Minnesota and Mary Elizabeth Lease of Kansas became national figures, and in that year's elections, Alliance candidates won numerous local elections in western states. In 1891, the Northern Alliance joined forces with the National Farmers' Alliance and Industrial Union (or Southern Alliance) headed by Dr. C. W. Macune of Texas. Together, they formed the People's Party, commonly known as the Populists. At its 1892 convention in Omaha, Nebraska, the party nominated former Union general James B. Weaver of Iowa for president and the former Confederate general James G. Field of Virginia as vice-president. The Populist platform called for the abolishment of national banks; the nationalization of railroads, telegraph, and telephone lines; a graduated income tax; a sub-treasury system of warehouses whereby farmers could secure better credit using stored crops as collateral; and the free and unlimited coinage of silver.[23] In the November election, Weaver came in a distant third behind Grover Cleveland, the Democratic victor, and his Republican opponent, Benjamin Harrison. Although Weaver failed to attract many voters in Chicago, the Populists did well in the West, carrying the silver states of Idaho, Nevada, and Colorado and capturing numerous state offices in Kansas, Nebraska, North Dakota, and Minnesota.[23]

After 1892, the silver issue became an increasingly important issue in national politics. To help pay off heavy loads of debt, farmers in the West and South favored the free and unlimited coinage of silver, which would put more money in circulation. Western mining interests also favored the free coinage of silver, believing it would

Established in 1848, the Chicago Board of Trade became the central market place for western grain. During the 1880s, western farmers protested that its middlemen dealers, along with the railroads, cut into their profits.

revive their industry, decimated by the repeal of the Sherman Silver Purchase Act, and help restore silver's former value of "sixteen to one" (the coinage rate of silver to gold) lowered by Congress in 1873. Although many Populists did not go along with all the arguments of the "silverites," they agreed that the government had an obligation to increase the amount of money in circulation, whatever its form.

When the stock market crashed in 1893, creating massive unemployment, the money question became a major story in newspapers and political journals. No publication, however, caught the public's attention like *Coin's Financial School,* published by William Hope Harvey of

Chicago in 1894. Originally from Virginia, Harvey had lived in the West, where he invested in ranching and mining. After the crash of 1893 wiped him out financially, he moved to Chicago. His book, which sold millions of copies, presented Dr. Coin, an imaginary character who delivered a series of lectures on the silver issue at the Art Institute. His "audience" included prominent Chicagoans such as Philip Armour, Potter Palmer, Marshall Field, John Farwell, and Joseph Medill of the *Chicago Tribune*.[24]

Using clear and simple terms, Coin, "the smooth little financier," instructed his "class" on the money question. He focused on the "Crime of 1873," when Congress devalued silver and left the gold dollar as the standard unit of monetary value. Although the act did not eliminate silver dollars, it reduced the amount of silver—"the people's money"—in circulation, while it made gold—"the money of the rich"—more valuable. Indebted western farmers were especially hurt. "A great sponge," Coin declared, referring to eastern creditors, "comes West twice a year and soaks up your money and takes it away." Coin identified England, the gold-based financial capital of the world, as the ultimate villain. "The gold standard will give England the commerce and wealth of the world," stated Coin, whereas "the bi-metallic [gold and silver] standard will make the U.S. the most prosperous nation on the globe."[25]

The silver movement reached a crescendo in 1896 when the Democratic Party nominated William Jennings Bryan, a Nebraska congressman, for president at its convention in Chicago. Bryan, who flirted with the doctrines of the Populist Party but never actually joined its ranks, mesmerized the convention with his famous "Cross of Gold" speech, in which he decried the exploitation of the poor, the West, and the South by eastern capitalists. "The great cities rest upon our broad and fertile prairies," declared Bryan, "Burn down your cities and leave our farms, and your cities will spring up again as if by magic; but destroy our farms and the grass will grow in the streets of every city in the country."[26]

To the dismay of many Populists, Bryan's candidacy emphasized the popular silver issue while downplaying other reforms. Other Populists feared that Bryan had stolen their issues, sounding the death knell of their own party. Despite these concerns, the Populist Party also nominated Bryan at their convention in St. Louis. In the November election, Bryan carried most western and southern states, but William McKinley, his well-financed Republican opponent, defeated him by nearly six hundred thousand votes. In Chicago, a Republican stronghold since 1860, Bryan ran well among industrial workers, but still lost by more than sixty-five thousand votes.[27] After the election of 1896, the Populist movement began to wane. A resurgent national economy in 1897 quelled agrarian fears and good times continued through World War I. Between 1900 and 1910, when around 60 percent of the country's entire population lived in rural areas, prices of agricultural products increased by nearly

The Free Silver movement took off in the 1890s. Above: William Hope Harvey of Chicago published Coin's Financial School *in 1894 as a series of "lectures" that favorably compared the silver standard to the gold. Below: A political handkerchief from the 1896 presidential campaign features Democratic nominee, William Jennings Bryan, and his running mate, Arthur Sewall, who ran on a campaign of free silver.*

half and the value of farm property doubled. Yet, most farmers, especially those in the more isolated West, remained suspicious of an economic system that favored big businesses and of middlemen who took a hefty percentage of every transaction.

Perhaps nowhere is the American farmer's discontent more evident than in the phenomenal growth of the mail-order industry. Farmers resented local merchants who sold a limited assortment of high-priced goods on credit. Two well-known Chicago firms, Montgomery Ward and Company and Sears, Roebuck & Company towered over all their competitors in tapping this huge market of disgruntled consumers. Montgomery Ward and

Company, established in 1872 by Aaron Montgomery Ward and his brother-in-law, George R. Thorne, identified itself as "The Original Grange Supply House." Ward had worked as a general-store manager and dry-goods salesman and knew first-hand of farmers' unhappiness with local merchants. He operated on a cash-only basis, buying goods from manufacturers and selling them directly to farmers, thus eliminating the middleman as well as poor credit risks. Buying and selling in great volume, Ward kept prices low and profits high.

Ward's product line included dry goods, clothing, shoes, toilet goods, jewelry and watches, Grange regalia, and a wide assortment of household and farm equip-

The Pullman Strike of 1894

Like the Great Railroad Strike of 1877, the Pullman Strike of 1894 interrupted trade between Chicago and the West by crippling the nation's transportation system. The origins of the Pullman Strike lay in the Panic of 1893, when an international economic downturn caused a run on the U.S. gold reserve and a major stock market crash. In response to these bad times, George Pullman, inventor of the railroad sleeping car, fired about one-third of his workforce at the Pullman Palace Car Works in Chicago and cut the wages of those who remained by 30 percent. He would not, however, lower the prices of food and housing in Pullman, the company town he had built for his employees on the city's far South Side.

On May 11, 1894, the local chapter of the American Railway Union (ARU) struck and, when Pullman refused arbitration, ARU's president, Eugene V. Debs, ordered a nationwide strike of all trains using Pullman cars. Railroad workers in the western part of the country responded to his order—from Ohio to California, sympathetic strikes occurred in twenty-seven states and territories. At first, the union seemed to have the upper hand, especially in Chicago, the nation's rail capital. But violence of questionable origin broke out in the city, and on July 6,

A cartoon from the July 14, 1894, issue of Harper's Weekly *depicts Eugene V. Debs blocking the passage of well-stocked trains during the Pullman Strike.*

President Grover Cleveland ordered two thousand troops into Chicago under the command of Gen. Nelson A. Miles. By mid-July, the strike had collapsed, broken by the presence of the military, the arrest of Debs, the lack of support from other national unions, and the unified position of railroad management. In the strike's aftermath, Debs advocated Socialism, convinced that its programs offered the only solutions to working peoples' problems.

Living far from local stores, western farmers became good customers of Chicago's mail-order industry. This 1894 catalog from Montgomery Ward and Company included photographs of its products, along with dozens of testimonials from satisfied customers.

ment. Ward's guaranteed customers that if they were not completely satisfied with their purchase, they could return it at no charge. The company grew steadily and by 1884 claimed to carry ten thousand items worth more than a half-million dollars.[28] For the next twenty years, Ward's remained the top mail-order house in America. Its chief competitors included Spiegel and May, Stern & Co., both of Chicago; and Sears, Roebuck & Company, founded by Richard Warren Sears of Minneapolis in 1886. Sears, a telegraph operator and railroad agent for the Minneapolis & St. Paul Railroad, began his remarkable career by selling watches to other railroad agents. In 1887, he moved his business, the R.W. Sears Watch Company, to Chicago and hired Alvah Curtis Roebuck, a watch repairman. At first, the company sold only diamonds, watch chains, and other jewelry, but it soon expanded to include sewing machines, furniture, dishes, clothing, and hundreds of other items. By 1895, the Sears catalog had more than five hundred pages, featuring an incredible array of consumer goods that generated three-quarters of a million dollars in business.

A natural-born salesman who could "sell a breath of fresh air," Sears promoted his company as one that "waged war" against manufacturers and dealers with low prices and "money back" guarantees. Enjoying the benefits of Rural Free Delivery (RFD), a newly created system that delivered mail directly to rural residents, Sears flooded the market with catalogs and promotions. In 1900, he developed a sales campaign that allowed farmers to receive and inspect products without paying a penny. Although it resulted in nine hundred thousand dollars worth of unclaimed—and therefore unpaid for—goods, the "Send No Money" campaign made Sears seem like a "real friend" of the farmer and helped it replace Ward's as the largest mail-order house in the country.[29]

While mail order flourished, it also generated controversy. Its critics dated back to the early 1870s, when the *Chicago Tribune* issued a warning: "Grangers Beware! Don't Patronize 'Montgomery Ward & Co.'—they are Dead-Beats."[30] Understandably, small merchants throughout the West vigorously opposed the mail-order industry, pressuring local newspapers to keep their advertisements out of circulation. In the early 1900s, the newly formed Home Trade

No. 22 MAIL OPENING AND MAIL AUDITING DEPARTMENTS. SEARS, ROEBUCK & CO., Chicago, Ill.

Each day, armies of clerks in Chicago's mail-order companies filled thousands of orders from customers. A stereograph card from the turn of the century presents a view of the mail opening and auditing room of Sears, Roebuck & Company.

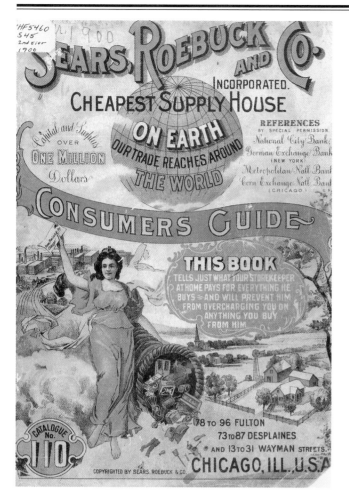

The front cover and a product page from the 1901 Sears, Roebuck & Company catalog features the densely crowded advertising style developed by Richard Sears himself. Sears appealed to its rural market with a central farm scene on the cover, but didn't forget its urban customers—the cover included a city view as well.

Leagues of America, an association that encouraged customers to trade in town, rather than order through the mail.

In Chicago, Thomas J. Sullivan, a writer for the American Press Association, became a leading opponent of mail-order with the publication of *Merchants and Manufacturers on Trial*, in which he charged: "War has been declared on the great catalog houses of Chicago and other cities by the 500,000 retail merchants of the West. In one of the most striking economic movements this country has ever known, the small dealers are fighting, as they say, for their lives." Sullivan went on: "The mammoth institutions, which employ thousands of workers, doing their business entirely through the medium of their bulky catalogs, spending no money in the community whence they derive annually millions of dollars of patronage are forcing increasing numbers of home merchants to the wall and, so their opponents claim, are 'making commercial graveyards of once prosperous towns.'"[31]

The attack on the mail-order industry reached its peak in 1910, when Congress held hearings on parcel post. Parcel post allowed for the direct mailing of packages through regular mail, rather than by freight or mail express. As expected, farmers, grangers, farmers' clubs, and labor unions supported parcel post, while small-town merchants, commercial clubs, and retail associations vigorously opposed it. Despite these pressures, Congress responded to the demands of the rural majority by approving parcel post in 1913. Parcel post further boosted mail order's phenomenal growth in the 1910s, boosting the combined sales of Sears and Ward's to $300 million in 1918.[32]

In addition to its economic impact, the phenomenal growth of Chicago's mail-order business, along with its other western industries—railroads, meatpacking, and agricultural machinery—reflected larger changes in American society. Between 1860 and 1920, the nation's population, which had increased from thirty-one million to ninety-four million people, became increasingly urban in nature; in 1860, nearly 90 percent of Americans lived in rural areas, but by 1920, 51 percent lived in urban areas of twenty-five hundred or more.[33] This dramatic shift in national demographics occurred chiefly because industrialization decreased the need for rural laborers, while increasing the need for urban factory workers. Indeed, this change had occurred in the West thirty years earlier, with more westerners living in urban areas than rural by 1890. As industrialization took hold, fewer Americans than ever before produced their own food, clothing, and shelter. Instead, they purchased basic necessities and an increasing number of luxury items in the marketplace, whether in town or through mail order. The forces responsible for this profound transformation of American society not only affected Chicago and the West, but transformed the United States into a major world power.

NOTES FOR CHAPTER FOUR: AN ECONOMIC EMPIRE

1. Louise C. Wade, *Chicago's Pride: The Stockyards, Packingtown, and Environs in the Nineteenth Century* (Urbana, Illinois: University of Illinois Press, 1987), 48; Jack Wing, *The Great Union Stock Yards of Chicago* (Chicago: n.p., 1865), 23.
2. Wade, *Chicago's Pride*, 55–56.
3. Ibid., 229; Richard White, "Animals and Enterprise," *The Oxford History of the West*, ed. Clyde A. Milner II, Carol A. O'Connor, and Martha A. Sandweiss (New York: Oxford University Press, 1994), 256.
4. J. Evetts Haley, *The XIT Ranch of Texas and the Early Days of The Llano Estacado* (Chicago: The Lakeside Press, 1929), 53–62.
5. Haley, *XIT Ranch*, 182–94.
6. *XIT Rules*.
7. Haley, *XIT Ranch*, 217–28.
8. John Clay, *My Life on the Range* (Chicago: privately printed, 1924), 322.
9. Ibid., 224.
10. Official Catalog, International Live Stock Exposition, (Chicago: P. F. Pettibone & Co., 1901), 10–11.
11. Ibid., 6.
12. Ibid., 87, 346–47.
13. Ibid., 14–15.
14. William T. Hutchinson, *Cyrus Hall McCormick, Harvest, 1856–1884* (New York: D. Appleton-Century Co., 1935), 522–56.
15. Ibid., 719–21.
16. Ibid., 328–30; *The Glad Hand Is the Right Hand* (Chicago: Rand, McNally & Co., 1898), back cover.
17. Louis M. Hacker, *The Course of American Economic Growth and Development* (New York: John Wiley & Sons, Inc., 1970), 227.
18. John D. Hicks, *The Populist Revolt, A History of the Farmers' Alliance and the People's Party* (Minneapolis: University of Minnesota Press, 1931), 98.
19. *The Western Rural*, October 15, 1881.
20. Ibid., 9–10.
21. Hacker, *The Course of American Economic Growth*, 232; *The Western Rural*, Dec. 27, 1884; February 9, 1884; January 3 and 17, 1885; March 7, 1885.
22. Hicks, *Populist Revolt*, 103; *The Western Rural*, October 15, 1887.
23. Hicks, *Populist Revolt*, 274.
24. William H. Harvey, *Coin's Financial School* (Chicago: Coin Publishing Company, 1894), 4–20.
25. Ibid., 121, 135.
27. *Chicago Tribune*, November 4, 1896.
28. Boris Emmet and John E. Jeuck, *Catalogues and Counters, A History of Sears, Roebuck & Co.* (Chicago: The University of Chicago Press, 1950), 19–22.
29. Ibid., 74.
30. *Chicago Tribune*, November 8, 1873.
31. Emmet and Jeuck, *Catalogues and Counters*, 156.
32. Ibid., 79, 82, 89, 196.
33. Ibid., 10–11.

Originally designed by Chicago publisher George Crofutt, American Progress *presents a mythical view of western history. With the "Star of Empire" on her forehead, a heavenly figure of enlightenment leads white settlers westward across the continent, displacing American Indians in the process.*

FIVE

Western Myth

From the beginning of its western adventure, Chicago helped create a popular, romantic mythology about the West that remains deeply ingrained in American culture and identity. Essentially, the myth depicts the West as a wild frontier tamed by heroic white settlers who overcame great danger and hardship to establish new homes for themselves and their families. The mythical West also includes "savage Indians" and "notorious outlaws" who are ultimately conquered by the civilizing forces of Christianity and democracy. With its emphasis on individualism, freedom, and the redemptive qualities of nature, America's western mythology embodies many elements of nineteenth century romanticism and builds upon the fanciful histories of earlier frontiersmen like Daniel Boone, Davy Crockett, and Kit Carson.

Western myth, like others throughout time, helps to unify and sustain a culture. Developed in the aftermath of a destructive civil war, it helped restore the country's belief in itself as an agent of civilization and progress. Enormously appealing to most Americans, the western myth also became an opportunity for clever entrepreneurs to make money.

Beginning in the 1860s, the railroad industry, headquartered in Chicago, championed the West as a land of breathtaking beauty and adventure. In sharp contrast to earlier descriptions of the West as a desert, the railroad industry promoted the West as a healthy respite from congested eastern cities, a place where weary urbanites could relax and restore themselves. To promote western tourism, railroads produced thousands of broadsides, travel guides, and advertisements. In a typical pamphlet

produced for the trade, the Chicago & North Western Railway glowingly described the many cities, towns, and natural wonders along its western routes. To attract a growing number of recreational hunters and sportsmen, the Chicago, Rock Island & Pacific Railway issued informative guides to the great hunting and fishing grounds of northern Iowa, central Minnesota, and eastern Dakota. During peak season, two daily express trains serviced these formerly remote areas, providing "every accommodation" for those taking their guns and dogs with them.[1]

Like the railroads, Chicago's publishing industry capitalized on the interest in western travel by issuing a plethora of travel guides, train schedules, and maps for tourists and settlers. Rand, McNally & Company, one of the country's largest publishing houses, printed numerous titles aimed at the western market, including *The Travelers' Hand Book to All Western Railways and Steamboat Lines*, *The Business Atlas of the Great Mississippi Valley and Pacific Slope*, and *The Illustrated Guide to Colorado, New Mexico, and Arizona*. All such guides portrayed western travel as a romantic adventure, a chance to escape the confines of civilization and visit a more natural world that would refresh and restore one's spirit.

Travel guides written by George A. Crofutt of Chicago epitomized the "art" of western travel writing. Originally from Connecticut, Crofutt had hauled supplies for the Union Pacific Railroad and compiled a city directory for Salt Lake City before moving to Chicago in 1869. His first book, the *Great Trans-Continental Railroad Guide*, contained a "full and authentic description of over five hundred cities, towns, villages, stations, government forts and camps, mountains, lakes, rivers, sulfur, soda and hot springs, scenery, watering places, [and] summer resorts." Crofutt told travelers where to "look for and hunt the buffalo, antelope, deer, and other game" and "where to go—how to go—and whom to stop with" while passing over the transcontinental railroad.[2]

An immediate success, Crofutt's book sold tens of thousands of copies and led to his publication of a series of western travel guides over the next twenty-three years.

Chicago railroads helped develop western tourism by publishing colorful advertisements, such as this Chicago & North Western broadside from 1887. To encourage business, railroads ran express trains that accommodated sportsmen's dogs.

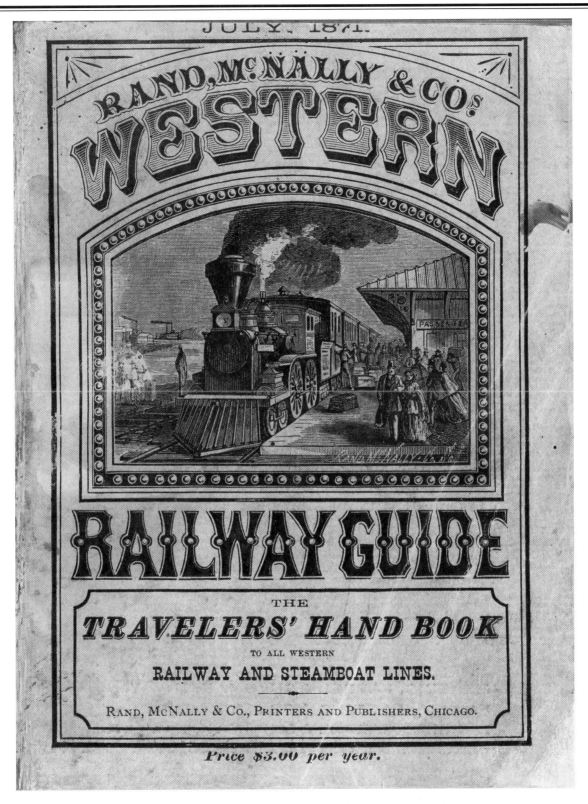

Based in Chicago, Rand, McNally & Company flourished as a result of western expansion. Each year, it printed an updated guide of train routes and schedules, along with connecting stagecoach and steamboat lines.

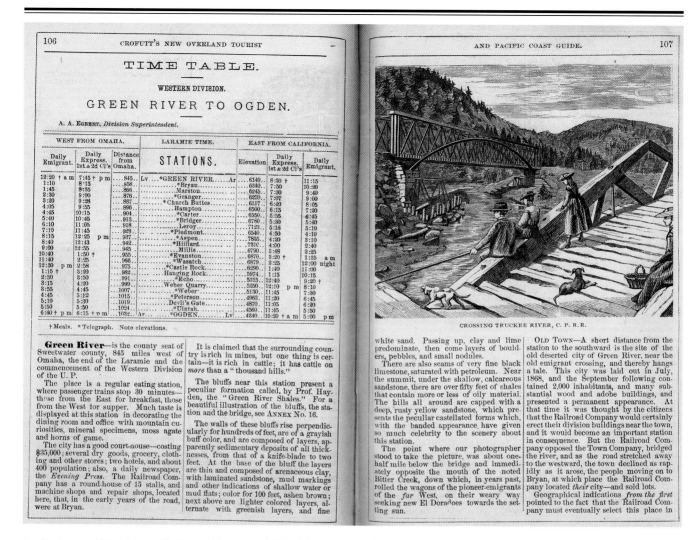

Beginning in 1878, George Crofutt of Chicago published the most popular western guide books in America until Rand, McNally bought him out in 1890. Filled with useful information, handsome illustrations and vivid descriptions, Crofutt's books stimulated western tourism.

Crofutt, who wrote most of the text, always invited his fellow-travelers to "lay aside all city prejudices and ways for the time; leave them here, and for once be natural while among nature's loveliest and grandest creations . . . above all forget everything but the journey." In 1890, Rand, McNally & Company took over Crofutt's business, publishing what became their most successful western guidebooks, *Crofutt's Overland Guide* and *Crofutt's Overland Tours*.[3]

To attract more travelers, railroads purchased luxurious cars made by the Pullman Palace Car Company of Chicago. Established in 1867 by George Mortimer Pullman, the company introduced a sleeping car with private berths that greatly improved upon the crude railway sleeping cars

then in operation. The Pullman Company also made lavish dining cars with their own kitchens and sumptuous parlor cars for lounging passengers. Furnished with upholstered seats, wooden cabinetry, and brass fixtures, and staffed by an attentive crew of exclusively African American porters and waiters, Pullman sleepers and diners provided luxurious accommodations for first-class passengers able to afford an extra $6.00 to $8.00 a day for a berth and between $1.00 and $1.50 for each meal.

In the late 1880s, the Pullman Company introduced a day and sleeping Tourist Car to accommodate the growing number of second-class travelers. Although less elaborately furnished than the palace cars, the tourist cars nonetheless provided travelers with pleasant accommodations. The day cars had wicker or leather seats and their own cooking facilities and ice chests for passenger use. Sleepers "fitted up complete with mattresses, curtains, blankets, pillows, etc." were staffed by uniformed porters who "look after the wants of the passengers." With fares less than half the cost of palace cars, tourist cars encouraged thousands of new travelers, families, and excursion parties to visit the West. While racked by poor employee relations and a bitter wage strike in 1894, the Pullman Company succeeded in making long-distance travel comfortable and affordable for the middle class as well as for the wealthy elite.[4]

Just as urbanites journeyed west, so did the West come east in various forms of popular entertainment. During the 1870s, Chicago newspapers frequently ran stories about the West that reinforced its romantic image. In reporting on Kansas in 1879, D. S. Covert, a special correspondent for the *Chicago Tribune*, wrote:

> The wheatfields are glorious with their golden waves of ripening grain; the corn is shooting rapidly, and is loud with the promise of the coming harvest; the prairies are alive with countless cattle and sheep, and not alone carpeted with its wealth of grass, but fragrant with flowers of every hue. The prairie-flowers of Kansas are wonderful for their brightness of color, their fragrance, and their great variety and delicacy of tint.[5]

Covert's description of settlers building new homes on the western frontier reflected a common assumption that those who worked hard would prosper:

> The humble 'dug out' in the side of the prairie-bluff, or the cabin of logs cut from the river-side, and piled with much labor, and plastered with mud, shall grow under diligent husbandry, and accretions of full barns and stock-yards, crowded with lowing herds, shall gather, and finally the well-built mansion shall replace the dug-out or the cabin, and the last days shall be a serene sunset and cloudless sky.[6]

In a typically romanticized account of western cow-boys, Covert wrote:

> cow-boys, while tending . . . their Texas cattle, which are almost as wild as buffalos, and as dangerous to a

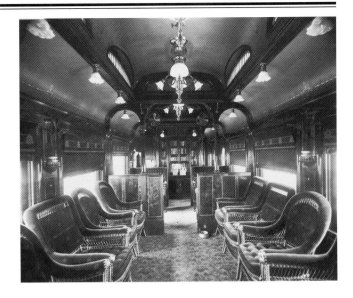

Although the Pullman Palace Car Company of Chicago became famous for first-class luxury, like that found in the parlor car pictured above, it made comfortable second-class cars as well. Below: An illustration from the July 18, 1891, issue of Harper's Weekly *depicts passengers gazing at the Rocky Mountains from its popular observation car.*

man on foot, are accustomed to sing a great deal to while away the lonely hours. . . . Sometimes, in the night, a thunder-clap or some strange sound, will start up the cattle in wild affright, and they will snort and paw the earth, and in a moment a wild rush and stampede would commence. But the cow-boys will spring up, and, while they loose and mount their ponies, they commence singing their old songs. The cattle, hearing the well-known and accustomed voices, will soon quiet down, thinking all is right, and resume their rest again.[7]

The Pullman Porters

An American legend, the Pullman Porters provided luxury service to millions of railroad passengers for over a century. For decades, this job was held exclusively by African Americans, who began working for the Pullman Palace Car Company in 1867, when the company was founded. At the time, racial barriers severely limited employment opportunities for African Americans, and so they accepted Pullman's low wages in exchange for a steady paycheck and fairly good job security.

Porters served first- and second-class passengers on the company's sleeping, dining, and lounge cars. As western travel increased around the turn of the century, the Pullman Company employed thousands of porters, becoming the largest single employer of African Americans in the nation. By serving passengers' needs, Pullman Porters revolutionized long-distance travel, which had once been uncomfortable and exhausting. Among the first blacks to attain an economic foothold in America, Pullman porters helped break down some social and racial barriers between whites and blacks. In 1925, a small group of Pullman Porters led by A. Philip Randolph established the Brotherhood of Sleeping Car Porters, which negotiated better wages and working conditions for its members.

African American attendants serving white middle- and upper-class passengers in Pullman dining cars, 1894.

In addition to creating romantic images of settlers and cowboys, Chicago newspapers also helped promote one of the most famous of all western legends, that of George Armstrong Custer. In the summer of 1874, William Curtis, special correspondent for the *Inter Ocean*, accompanied Custer's expedition to the Black Hills. On July 9, Curtis wrote:

> He is a great man—a noble man is General Custer . . . I came here expecting to find a big-whiskered, swearing, ranting, drinking trapper, and I found instead a slender, quiet gentleman, with a face as fair as a girl's, and manners as gentle and courtly as the traditional prince. Hunting for the drunken raider, I found a literary gentleman, in his library. . . . His guest for four days, I never sat with a more courteous host, or generous entertainer, or polished conversationalist. . . . General Custer does not drink . . . does not swear . . . does not smoke . . . But what, some one will ask, are his vices? His soldiers will tell you he has none.[8]

When Custer met defeat at the Battle of the Little Bighorn, Chicago newspapers, like others across the country, carried reports that greatly distorted reality. The *Inter Ocean* described the following story as an eyewitness account, even though no white person survived the battle.

> General Custer and his five companies took position on a ridge in the center of the Indian camp, cut off from access to water, and there fought desperately all day long, a conspicuous mark for the savage marksmen all around. At last, when half his command had been killed, he called on those that remained to follow him, and dashed boldly through the red devils. It was running the gauntlet of at least 2,000 rifles for the whole distance. His men did not follow him, and when he got through he found himself alone with a single Crow Indian, one of his scouts. He would not leave his men to perish, alone, and turned to go back, but the Crow, recognizing that such a movement would be fatal, grabbed his horse and implored him not to go back. Custer only laughed and, putting the reins of his horse between his teeth, with a revolver in each hand, he gave a wild cheer, and dashed back through the hell of

smoke and flying bullets. As if by a miracle he reached the remnants of his command, which was now reduced to forty men. Calling on these survivors again to follow him, which the example and success of his former charge disposed them to do, he led them from their place of peril over the path of his solitary charge. That was the last seen of them until the battle was over.[9]

Such imaginative reports, along with hundreds of dime novels churned out by hack writers, captivated a broad segment of the American public. When the famous dime novelist Ned Buntline adapted the western genre to the stage, the results were nothing short of phenomenal. On December 16, 1872, Buntline opened a three-act play at Nixon's Amphitheatre in Chicago. Entitled *The Scouts of the Prairie*, Buntline's play starred himself, the famous Indian scout Buffalo Bill Cody, John B. "Texas Jack" Omohundro, an ex-scout of the Confederate cavalry, and Mlle. Morlacchi, an Italian-born actress who played an Indian maiden named "Dove Eye." On opening night, both Buffalo Bill and Texas Jack forgot their lines but delighted the audience by ad-libbing stories of their western adventures. A rousing fight scene followed, with the heroes battling a group of Indians played by poorly made-up white actors. More Indian fighting, and not much else, comprised the next two acts.[10]

Chicago's drama critics roundly panned the show. The *Tribune*'s drama critic wrote that the play "purports to be a vivid picture of life in the Western wilds, and is such to a certain extent—as much so are the average sensational novels on the same subject, and, like the latter, full of inconsistencies." The *Inter Ocean* wryly commented: "There is a well-founded rumor that Ned Buntline, who played the part of Gale Durg in last night's performance, wrote the play in which Buffalo Bill and Texas Jack appeared, taking only four hours to complete the task. The question naturally arises: what was he doing all that time?"[11]

Despite these bad reviews, *The Scouts of the Prairie* drew greater crowds than any other act in town, including a minstrel show at Myer's Theatre and *Julius Caesar* at Aiken's. More than two thousand people attended each performance of the play during its four-day run. As noted

by the *Inter Ocean*, the play attracted a working-class audience that was not "what the ordinary critic would stigmatize as select and cultivated; but it was very appreciative, yes, enthusiastic." Audiences delighted in the "hairbreadth escapes, the thrilling adventures of Indian life, the heroic scout, the splendid Indian maid, the terrible redskin . . . here they have been promised a chance of seeing the actual heroes of whom they had long read and dreamed."[12]

After leaving Chicago, the play toured to St. Louis, Cincinnati, and New York. Enormously popular, *The Scouts of the Prairie* inspired a spate of western dramas in large cities. More importantly, it launched Buffalo Bill Cody's remarkable career in show business. Of all the members of the small troupe, Cody stood out as a natural star. A critic for the *New York World* described him as having "a curious grace and a certain characteristic charm that pleases the beholders. He is a remarkably handsome fellow on stage, and the lithe, springy step, the round western voice, the utter absence of anything like stage art, won for him the good will of an audience."[13]

After staging several successful melodramas, Cody organized an outdoor show featuring live animals and real cowboys and Indians. Entitled *The Wild West, Rocky Mountain and Prairie Exhibition*, Cody's show debuted in Omaha, Nebraska, on May 17, 1883. While Cody couldn't claim to be the first to stage an outdoor western show, he is the one who made it work. A tremendous success, Cody's first national tour ended in Chicago where Cody asked Nate Salsbury, a well-known showman, to become his partner. For nearly twenty years, Salsbury's astute business sense and theatrical experience brought order to the large and often unruly troupe of performers.

In May 1885, Cody and Salsbury brought an expanded version of their production to Chicago. Once again, the city gave Cody an enthusiastic welcome. On the first day of its two-week run, forty thousand people showed up at West Side Driving Park, which had seats for only half that number. Adults paid a fifty-cent admission fee, while children got in for a quarter. To open the show, one of Cody's performers rode a wild steer over from the Union Stock Yards. Members of the press, treated by Cody and Salsbury to a sumptuous roast-beef barbecue dinner the day before, lauded the show in the daily papers.[14]

A master of popular entertainment, Buffalo Bill Cody hired performers with "star quality." To make his show appear more authentic, Cody employed real cowboys, sharpshooters, and more than a hundred Plains Indians. Opposite: Sitting Bull toured with Cody's show in 1887. Above: a press pass for the 1885 Wild West show in Chicago. Below: An image of Annie Oakley from the 1893 program.

Cody's show contrasted sharply with Chicago newspaper stories describing drought in Kansas, ranchers in the Texas Panhandle trying to block cattle drives from the state's southern region, and Geronimo's raids in New Mexico and Arizona. But Cody's show did not attempt to create a realistic portrait of the West. Instead, it presented a Western spectacle in twenty acts that included trick shooting by Annie Oakley and a living tableaux of the "Phases of Indian Life." The program concluded with "The Attack on the Settler's Cabin," in which Buffalo Bill defeats a group of "marauding Indians."[15]

Cody and Salsbury claimed their show presented the "most completely-appointed delegation of frontiersmen and Indians that ever visited the East." Like other popular entertainers of the time, they billed their product as "new, startling, and instructive." While the Buffalo Bill show did little more than reinforce western mythology and racial stereotypes, it drew tremendous crowds wherever it played, including Europe.

An international star, Cody did not return to Chicago until the 1893 World's Columbian Exposition. Fair organizers, however, refused to include Cody because they considered his show entertainment, not education. Renting a fourteen-acre site across from the main entrance of the exposition, Cody opened his show a month before the fair. No longer just a "Wild West show" but an international extravaganza, *Buffalo Bill's Wild West and Congress of Rough Riders* featured elaborately costumed cavalrymen and acrobats from Europe and the Middle East. The show also included Annie Oakley; Chief Rain In The Face, who claimed to have killed Custer at Little Bighorn; and the Ghost Dancers Kicking Bear and Short Bull. Thanks to the show's reputation and some shrewd publicity, including a one-thousand-mile cowboy race from Chadron, Nebraska, Cody's show consistently drew crowds as large as eighteen thousand people. By the close of the fair, Cody and his associates had cleared more than $1 million.[16]

Obviously, American audiences in 1893 still enjoyed western legends but, as Cody's elaborate program demonstrates, they needed something more to hold their attention. Even Cody himself must have realized that the Wild West of his youth, and that of the nation's youth, had vanished. As noted by the U.S. Census Bureau in 1890 and by Frederick Jackson Turner in an address to the American Historical Association in Chicago in July 1893, the long-cherished American frontier no longer existed.

As Turner observed, America *had* changed. Since the close of the Civil War a mere thirty years before, America had grown from a young, predominantly agrarian country to one of the most powerful industrialized nations in the world. With large exhibition halls filled with modern machinery and mass-produced goods, the 1893 world's fair celebrated America's industrial progress, consciously comparing it to the more "primitive" American Indian, African, and Asian cultures represented in the Anthropology Hall.

Essanay Studios, established in Chicago in 1907, produced many early western movies, most notably the popular Broncho Billy *series starring Gilbert M. Anderson. A bioscope camera (right) used by Essanay Studios, c. 1910; Broncho Billy filming in the studio, c. 1910 (below).*

America's western mythology, however, continued to capture the public's imagination, taking on new life with the birth of motion pictures. Two early film companies based in Chicago, Selig Polyscope Studio and Essanay Studios, produced hundreds of highly popular westerns. In 1904, William Selig made the first movie filmed in Chicago, *Trapped by Bloodhounds; or, A Lynching in Cripple Creek*. His first westerns were shot on back streets and empty lots in Chicago, but in 1906, to satisfy audience demand for more realistic settings, he sent a small company of actors to film on location in Montana and California.

One of Selig's early western stars was Tom Mix. A real cowboy who starred in Wild West shows, Mix began his movie career in 1909 when Selig hired him to handle stock and act as a safety man for *Ranch Life in the Great Southwest*, billed as a documentary about ranching but actually a filmed series of rodeo events. After demonstrating his trick-riding skills, Mix won a part in the movie as a bronco buster. Mix went on to star in a series of westerns usually shot in Prescott, Arizona, at the Diamond S Ranch, which Mix received as part of his contract with Selig. A flamboyant personality who emulated Buffalo Bill Cody, Mix wore elaborate western clothing and a trademark broad-brimmed white hat. Between 1910 and 1917, Mix appeared in over two hundred western movies, including *Sagebrush Tom* and *The Heart of Texas Ryan*.[17]

Gilbert M. Anderson also began his movie career with Selig. A former vaudeville actor whose real name was Max Aaronson, Anderson had never ridden a horse before his movie career, but became America's most popular cowboy hero. He starred in several movies with Selig's company, including *The Girl from Montana* and *The Bandit King*, but left in 1907 to establish Essanay Studios with George Spoor. The company, with a name formed

from the first initials of each man's last name, had offices on Clark Street in downtown Chicago and a studio at 1333–45 West Argyle Street.

After several routine westerns, Anderson created the character of "Broncho Billy," whose popularity led to a series of 375 western films made between 1908 and 1915. Anderson shot most of these films on location in Niles Canyon, California, south of Oakland. Inexpensively produced for about eight hundred dollars apiece, each

Top left: a Broncho Billy advertisement from the Essanay News, *July 1, 1914. Below: Trick rider Tom Mix, who worked for the Selig Polyscope Studio of Chicago, became one of the most popular silent movie stars in America.*

Trying to salvage a flagging career, Cody made a movie for Chicago's Essanay Studios in 1913. Entitled The Indian Wars, *it re-created Cody's early adventures as an Army scout, as well as the tragic events at Wounded Knee.*

western grossed around fifty thousand dollars, making Anderson and Spoor wealthy men.[18]

Both the Tom Mix and Broncho Billy films typically followed a melodramatic plot in which the star battled outlaws and won the affections of a lovely girl. In *Broncho Billy and the Bandits*, Alice Matthews, daughter of the express agent in Red Rock, Arizona, is at home alone with her sick mother, guarding a box full of money. She mistakenly identifies Broncho Billy as the notorious "Arizona Kid" and locks him up in the storeroom. When the real bandits show up, Alice realizes her mistake and releases Broncho Billy, who deftly disarms the gang when they come crashing through the door.[19]

In 1913, Anderson's personal hero, the aging Buffalo Bill Cody, approached him with an idea for a film. Since the early 1900s, dwindling audiences, financial woes, and personal problems had plagued Cody, eroding his status as a showman and leaving him nearly bankrupt. Facing stiff competition from western movies, Cody decided to try his hand at the new medium, forming the Colonel W. F. Cody

Historical Pictures Company. Under the auspices of Essanay, Cody made one film—a documentary about the Indian Wars filmed on location at the Pine Ridge Indian reservation in South Dakota. Entitled *The Indian Wars Refought* or *The Wars for Civilization in America*, Cody's film starred himself, retired Gen. Nelson A. Miles, the United States Cavalry, and dozens of Sioux Indians. For its climax, the actors recreated the tragic events of Wounded Knee.[20]

Held back by the studio for six months, Cody's film eventually played a limited engagement. Opinions of the film varied according to the viewer's own perspective. Gen. Charles King, the film's author and a veteran of the Indian campaigns, described it as "the most wonderful spectacle ever produced," while Chauncey Yellow Robe, a Sioux Indian, attacked Cody's film in a speech to the Society of American Indians:

> Women and children and old men of my people, my relatives, were massacred with machine guns by the soldiers of this Christian nation while the fighting men were away. It was not a glorious battle and I think these two men [Cody and Miles] would be glad they were not there. But no, they want to be heroes for moving pictures.[21]

Whatever its merits, *The Indian Wars* failed to reverse Cody's financial fortunes and four years later he died in poverty. Chicago's movie studios declined during the same time period. In 1915, Essanay lost its biggest star, Charlie Chaplin, over a contract dispute, and Gilbert Anderson sold his shares of company stock to Spoor in order to become an independent producer. Courtroom battles over patent infringements and monopolization, increased competition, and the movement of the movie industry to California all contributed to Essanay's closing its doors in 1917. Selig's company experienced similar difficulties and sold off the last of its business in 1919.[22]

Although Chicago's position as a film center faded, western mythology lived on in Hollywood films and television programs produced later in the the twentieth century. For many Americans, the "Wild West" remains a powerful symbol of freedom and adventure, even though it disappeared long ago.

NOTES FOR CHAPTER FIVE: WESTERN LEGENDS

1. *Hunting and Fishing on the Lines of the Great Rock Island and Albert Lea Routes* (Chicago: J.M.W. Jones Stationery and Printing Co., n.d.), 28.

2. *Crofutt's New Overland Tourist and Pacific Coast Guide* (Chicago: The Overland Publishing Company, 1878), title page; J. Valerie Fifer, *American Progress: The Growth of the Transport, Tourist, and Information Industries in the Nineteenth Century West* (Chester, Connecticut: The Globe Pequot Press, 1988), 16–22.

3. Fifer, *American Progress,* 186–87, 326–31.

4. *Crofutt's New Overland Tourist,* 34; Fifer, *American Progress,* 205–07, 303, 403.

5. *Chicago Tribune,* July 4, 1879.

6. Ibid.

7. Ibid.

8. *Chicago Inter Ocean,* July 9, 1874.

9. Ibid., August 4, 1876.

10. *Chicago Tribune,* Dec. 17, 1872; Jay Monaghan, *The Great Rascal: The Exploits of The Amazing Ned Buntline* (New York: Little, Brown and Company, 1952), 19–22.

11. *Chicago Inter Ocean,* December 17, 1872.

12. Ibid., Dec. 19, 1872.

13. Henry Blackman Sell and Victor Weybright, *Buffalo Bill and The Wild West* (New York: Oxford Press, 1955), 103.

14. *Chicago Tribune,* May 19, 1885.

15. Buffalo Bill's Wild West Program, 1885, 2.

16. *Buffalo Bill's Wild West and Congress of Rough Riders of the World* (Chicago: The Blakely Printing Co., 1893).

17. Kevin Brownlow, *The War, the West, and the Wilderness* (New York: Alfred A. Knopf, 1979), 305–7.

18. Charles A. Jahant, "Chicago: Center of the Silent Film Industry," *Chicago History,* vol. 3, no. 3, Spring-Summer 1974, 45–53.

19. *Broncho Billy and the Bandits,* starring Broncho Billy, Essanay Studios, 1912; *The Moving Picture World,* vol. 12, April–June 1912, 356.

20. *Essanay News,* vol. 2, no. 10, Dec. 24, 1913.

21. Brownlow, *The War,* 235, 249.

Cowboys of the XIT Ranch, c. 1910.

Epilogue

View of the XIT Ranch, c. 1910.

As the nation's most critical phase of western expansion drew to a close in the late 1910s, the relationship between Chicago and the West began to change. In terms of transportation, Chicago remained the nation's gateway to the West, with an established network of railroad lines. Immigration quotas during World War I, however, slowed the rate of migration and fewer people moved west. Economically, Chicago maintained its position as the economic capital of the West, but cities such as Omaha, Kansas City, Fort Worth, and Denver became increasingly competitive. As the city became more urban and less tied to its agrarian past and regional neighbors, Chicago became less involved in western politics and aligned itself more with the interests of big business and eastern cities. Culturally, Chicago became more sophisticated and lost much of its western identity. Similarly, the West became a settled region with its own civilities and it too, seemed far removed from its not so distant past.

Thus, by World War I, Chicago and the West no longer enjoyed the same relationship that had built each of them into modern places. But together, they belonged to a powerful nation that would soon become a prominent player on the global stage.

Illustrations

PREFACE
4, CHS, ICHi-29519

INTRODUCTION
6, CHS, ICHi-29842

ACROSS THE CONTINENT
10, Oakland Museum of California, Oakland, CA, Russell #227; 11, CHS, ICHi-29779; 13, CHS, ICHi-10097; 14, CHS, ICHi-06861; 15, CHS, from *Biographical Sketches of the Leading Men of Chicago* (1876); 16, CHS, ICHi-14973; 17 top, CHS, ICHi-29786; 17 bottom, CHS, ICHi-29787; 18, CHS, ICHi-22523; 19 left, CHS, 1901.1; 19 right, Courtesy of Mrs. James F. Hunnewell (Eleanor Wheeler McClurg) and Mrs. Charles S. Potter (Barbara Ogden McClurg); 20, CHS, 1932.97; 21, CHS, *Reports of Explorations and Surveys to Ascertain the Most Practicable and Economical Route for a Railroad from the Mississippi River to the Pacific Ocean*, (1855–60); 22, CHS, ICHi-29658; 23 top, CHS, ICHi-29788; 23 bottom, 1920.53ab; 24, CHS, from Hartley, *Sun Pictures of Rocky Mountain Scenery* (1870); 26, Dallam-Hartley Counties Historical Association, Inc., 87-689-1B

INDUSTRIAL CONQUEST
27 left, CHS, ICHi-29655; 27 right, CHS, ICHi-29656; 28 top, CHS, from Andreas, *A History of Chicago*, vol. 3 (1884); 28 bottom, CHS, from Chicago, Rock Island & Pacific Railway, *Hunting and Fishing Grounds and Facilities for Healthful Sport* (n.d.); 29 top, CHS, ICHi-29654; 29 bottom, CHS, ICHi-29776; 30–31, CHS, ICHi-29809; 31 right, CHS, ICHi-29833; 32, National Anthropological Archives, Smithsonian Institution, 2856:4; 33, CHS, 1931.6; 34 left, CHS, ICHi-29662; 34 right, CHS, ICHi-29661; 35–38, CHS, "New Map of the Chicago and North Western Railway and Its Connections"; 39 top, CHS, ICHi-29773; 39 bottom, CHS, 1952.278ab; 40 left and right, Batavia Depot Museum, Batavia, IL; 41 left and right, CHS, from *Descriptive Catalogue of U.S. Wind Engine & Pump Co.* (1878); 42 top, Longmont Museum, Longmont, CO, B.59.57, Box2B; 42 bottom, Panhandle-Plains Historical Museum, Canyon, TX, AER-24; 43, Panhandle-Plains Historical Museum, Canyon, TX, AER-1; 44 top and bottom, Batavia Depot Museum, Batavia, IL; 45 top, CHS, ICHi-29651; 45 bottom, Longmont Museum, Longmont, CO, A.84.16, Box 26; 46 top, CHS, ICHi-29653; 46 bottom, CHS, from *Lyman Bridges Building Materials and Ready Made Houses* (1870); 47 all, Ellwood House Museum, De Kalb, IL; 48, Longmont Museum, Longmont, CO; 49 top, Longmont Museum, A.47.3, Box 3349; 49 bottom, Longmont Museum, 73.109.676, Box 1; 50, Longmont Museum, 80.42.34, Box 2 oversize

WAR WITHOUT
52, Denver Public Library, F27701; 54 top, CHS, ICHi-29783; 54 bottom, New York State Library, Albany, NY; 55 top, CHS-29841; 55 bottom, National Park Service, Little Bighorn Battlefield National Monument, Crow Agency, MT; 56, Newberry Library, Chicago, IL, Graff 4326; 57, Massachusetts State Historical Society, Boston, MA; 58 top, Montana Historical Society, Helena, MT, 943-884; 58 bottom, National Archives and Records Administration, Washington, D.C., 111-SC-87407; 59 left, CHS, from *Descriptive Catalogue of Photographs of North American Indians*, vol. 2 (1877), ICHi-29679; 59 right, National Anthropological Archives, Smithsonian Institution, Washington, D.C., 1380-A; 60, South Dakota State Historical Society, Pierre, SD, Mary Collins Collection, H-80-14; 61, National Archives and Records Administration, Washington, D.C., 77-HQ-264-809; 62 left, Newberry Library, Chicago, IL; 62 right, CHS, ICHi-29659; 63 top left, CHS, ICHi-29660; 63 bottom left, Newberry Library; 63 right, National Archives and Records Administration, Washington, D.C., 111-SC-85727; 65 all, private collection; 66, National Archives and Records Administration, Washington, D.C., 111-SC-85791; 67, CHS, 1989.624, box 1, folder 8; 68 top, CHS, 1989.624, box 1, folder 7; 68 bottom, Colorado Historical Society, Denver, CO, F-2562

AN ECONOMIC EMPIRE

70, State Historical Society of Wisconsin, Madison, WI, McCormick-International Harvester Collection; 71 top, CHS, ICHi-19107; 71 bottom, CHS, G1987.00624 N0070, neg. no. 26; 72 top, CHS, ICHi-29764; 72 bottom, Courtesy of A.C. & F., St. Charles, Missouri, from the collection of Tracy Jones; 73 top, CHS, 1978.154.5; 73 middle, ICHi-29808; 73 bottom, Courtesy of the family of Mr. Charles Potter, past president of the Union Stock Yards; 74 left, Newberry Library; 74 right, CHS, ICHi-29836; 75 top, CHS, 1923.81; 75 bottom left, CHS, ICHi-29790; 75 bottom right, CHS, ICHi-29789; 76 top, CHS, ICHi-29774; 76 bottom, CHS, ICHi-29626; 77 top left, CHS, ICHi-01622; 77 top right, CHS, 1976.205; 77 bottom left, CHS, 1956.355ab; 77 bottom right, CHS, 1960.232c; 78, CHS, ICHi-29620; 79, CHS, from *Buffalo Bill's Wild West and Congress of Rough Riders*; 80 top, CHS, ICHi-29625; 80 bottom, CHS, ICHi-29775; 81, CHS, ICHi-25852; 82 top, Dallam-Hartley Counties Historical Association, Inc., 1992-69-14; 82 middle, Courtesy of the family of Mr. Charles Potter, past president of the Union Stock Yards; 82 bottom, Panhandle-Plains Historical Museum, Canyon, TX; 83, CHS, from *My Life on the Range* (1924); 84, CHS, from *International Live Stock Exposition* (1909); 86–87 and 88 top and bottom, State Historical Society of Wisconsin, McCormick–International Harvester Collection; 89 top, CHS, from *Chicago Illustrated Graphic News*, February 23, 1888; 89 bottom, CHS, from *The Western Rural*, June 21, 1879; 91, CHS, ICHi-29619; 92 top, CHS, ICHi-29827; 92 bottom, CHS, ICHi-29807; 93, CHS, ICHi-29640; 94, CHS, ICHi-29635; 95, CHS, ICHi-23478; 96 left, CHS, ICHi-29623; 96 right, CHS, ICHi-29638

WESTERN MYTH

98, Autry Museum of Western Heritage, Los Angeles, CA; 100, CHS, ICHi-29627; 101, CHS, ICHi-29826; 102, CHS, from *Crofutt's New Overland Tourist and Pacific Coast Guide*, vol. 2 (1879–80), ICHi-29622; 103 top, Montana Historical Society, Helena, MT, H-4765, Elliot W. Hunter, photographer; 103 bottom, CHS, ICHi-29624; 104, CHS, from *Crofutt's New Overland Tourist Guide* (1878–79); 106, CHS, ICHi-29617; 107 top, CHS, tickets from Buffalo Bill's Wild West Show; 107 bottom, CHS, from program for Buffalo Bill's Wild West Show (1893); 108 top, CHS, ICHi-29806; 108 bottom, CHS, ICHi-16886; 109 top, CHS,from *Essanay News*, July 1, 1914; 109 bottom, CHS; 110, CHS, XG1981:021, Essanay Box 4

EPILOGUE

112, Dallam-Hartley Counties Historical Association, Inc., 77-250-14; 113, Panhandle-Plains Historical Museum, Canyon, TX Ph/1/832/537

Lenders

The following institutions and individuals generously loaned artifacts for the exhibition *Go West! Chicago and American Expansion.*

Batavia Depot Museum, Batavia, Illinois

Buffalo Bill Historical Center, Cody, Wyoming

Buffalo Bill Memorial Museum, Golden, Colorado

Chicago Board of Trade, Chicago, Illinois

Dallam-Hartley Counties Historical Association, Inc., Dalhart, Texas

Ellwood House Museum, De Kalb, Illinois

Lois K. and Richard D. Howe

Mrs. James F. Hunnewell (Eleanor Wheeler McClurg)

Tracy P. Jones

Library of Congress, Washington, D.C.

Longmont Museum, Longmont, Colorado

Museum of Texas Tech University, Lubbock, Texas

National Archives and Records Administration, Washington, D.C.

National Archives and Records Administration— Great Lakes Region, Chicago, Illinois

National Museum of American History, Smithsonian Institution, Washington, D.C.

Newberry Library, Chicago, Illinois

Panhandle-Plains Museum, Canyon, Texas

Family of Charles S. Potter, past president of the Union Stock Yards

Mrs. Charles S. Potter (Barbara Ogden McClurg)

State Historical Society of North Dakota, Bismarck, North Dakota

State Historical Society of Wisconsin, Madison, Wisconsin

W. H. Over State Museum, Vermillion, South Dakota

Index